ACKNOWLEDGEMENTS

I would like to thank my friends, especially John Stewart for his editing skills and steady encouragement; Graham England for his judicious advice and enthusiasm; and Mario Moscardini for rescuing the cover and for all the insights that I have claimed as my own.

Clive Hewat, my editor at Mainstream.

Mr Jerôme Bureau of *L'Equipe* for the long excerpt on the millennial Tour of Flanders which begins Chapter 16 – Merci.

Mr Robert Garbutt of *Cycling Weekly* for permission to reprint three articles which form the basis of Chapters 5, 7 and 16.

The quote from 'The Toughest Sport' in Chapter 2 appears © *The Economist Newspaper Ltd.* (11 February 1995).

BIKIE

A LOVE AFFAIR WITH
THE RACING BICYCLE

CHARLIE WOODS

MAINSTREAM
PUBLISHING

EDINBURGH AND LONDON

Reprinted 2008

First published in Great Britain in 2001 by
MAINSTREAM PUBLISHING COMPANY (EDINBURGH) LTD
7 Albany Street
Edinburgh EH1 3UG

Reprinted 2002, 2004

ISBN 9781840186574

A catalogue record for this book is available from the British Library

Typeset in Amphion and Giovanni
Printed and bound in Great Britain by
Cox & Wyman Ltd

Contents

Only the gaze that is turned backward can bring us forward, for the gaze that is turned forward leads us backward.

Novalis
(1722–1801)

1. Equipment Fetishists

Chris Brown rode a 'Dilecta', it was electric blue with white box-panelling; the tubing wasn't 531 double-butted and the lugs were nondescript; it didn't have a wrap-over seat cluster or even Simplex ends, but it was undeniably French and that made it a hothouse bloom amongst the hardy perennials of '50s Shepherd's Bush. To gild the orchid further, he had Bartali brake levers with finger indentations on South-of-France bars, and his wheels were secured by Huret wingnuts of phosphor bronze – details which itched the palms of schoolboy covetousness.

The fabled machine wasn't new of course, chance had delivered it to him second-hand and this element of good fortune conferred the aura of a minor miracle. We would gather round it, parked against the hedge, and worship its form and substance; divine providence had sent us this emblem of a higher, more magnificent design. The old chipped transfer with its stars, and the tiny lettering in the bottom corner: *marque déposée*, was like the primitive script on a sacred icon, words of such profundity that they were taken completely on trust – never questioned, never even discussed. It was a favour to be allowed room at these gatherings and by my regularity and fervour there I rose to the position of chief acolyte. And my dedication did not go without its indirect rewards. At school I was able to let drop that my friend owned a French bike and the name alone carried sufficient weight to boost my standing. We were all, of course, brothers of the wheel.

Chris was a year older so naturally I was in his shadow

anyway. Our tyre tracks had crossed in the Cubs when I needed every glimmer of reflected glory that I could soak up. All that stood between me and shanks' pony was an old sit-up-and-beg with rod brakes that I'd rescued from a bombsite. Anything like status was out of the question until the arrival of my first new bike, a Dawes Clansman with three-speed Benelux, GB brakes, Williams chainset and Lycett saddle. My Dad, recently returned from Australia wearing a large fedora and a gaberdine mac, asked me where we might make the purchase.

'Newton's,' I said without a moment's hesitation. It was the Holy of Holies of local cycling; the sort of place we would hang around on a Saturday afternoon just to see the clubmen come and go, examine their 'irons', and then pop down to again on Sunday to get a thorough look in the window.

We were tireless window shoppers. There was Algurn's and France-Sport in Chiswick, Les Scales' on the other side of Shepherd's Bush Green and then back up to Acton for the boss's emporium – it was a good afternoon's work to get round the lot. They didn't change much, those windows, but we always found something fresh – just the glimpse of a cotterless chainset or a CO_2 pump would be enough to lift us for the day. Newton's window was probably the least changed of all, but he was renowned as a frame-builder and it was the evidence of his handiwork that held out an irresistible attraction. One display would be reserved for an example of his bespoke skill, a single frame shining in its unadorned brilliance like a diamond. We were especially drawn to its lugwork; the sleeves which served as joints to the tubing brought together high technology and decorative flourish, they were the crowning glory of the builder's art. Long study had made each one of us a connoisseur of lugs.

A red-letter day had dawned when you could actually go into Newton's to make a purchase, but to buy a whole bike was tantamount to an audience with the mayor.

W.P. – Bill to the elect – was very unlike a civic dignitary however, more of a sergeant major. He tended to march around and shout which was difficult since his shop, although big on the outside, was so cluttered with bikes and counters that there was barely room for three people to gather. He did his spiel – more for my old man's benefit than mine admittedly – but I'd heard it all before anyway. I wanted to talk curly stays and scroll lugwork, I longed to plumb the mysteries of that notice which offered: 'Frames built to customer's own specifications.' I dreamed of the spells to be woven around angles and fork-rake and measured them against what met my ears: the burdens of the small businessman, the unpredictability of trade.

My Clansman was a pleasing enough colour, bright yellow (evidence in later years that I shared the same taste as one of the deities of the sport), but it only had twenty-six-inch wheels – and not even high pressure. It did, though, put me on an equal footing with Chris and his friend John McGrath. John had a Dayton, which were rumoured to crack at the head tube and deposit riders onto the tar and pebbles (the way they renewed the roads in those days). He scorned these libels by shuddering his bike with his straight handlebars just to show that for all its whippiness it would not break. These – the handlebars – were the only blemish on an otherwise impeccable profile. He had the great distinction of a four-speed gear, a Simplex, the nearest you could get to that vast divide where the gauge narrowed and you steamed away to the fabulous heights of a five block and that heaven of heavens – a double clanger. He even sported high pressures, but nothing could budge his adherence to straight handlebars. Drops were, of course, *de rigueur* for a serious aspirant, but no argument or chiding could dissuade him. We had to fall short of open derision because he was formidably hefty and could beat us hollow at any of the competitive disciplines: sprinting, hill climbing and slow-bicycle races.

We began to go out on a Sunday, exploring the Great West Road until we reached the airport, and then on to Windsor; after which the Sunday run was firmly established.

Somewhere along the road McGrath fell by the wayside – the

prophecy of his handlebars fulfilling itself – while Chris and I pursued our explorations until we hit upon Guildford, and that became our favourite excursion. At Thames Ditton you really felt that you were in the country, and a few testing climbs began to rear up, culminating in the narrow high street with its strange, almost medieval clock. On then to Lyon's Teashop where you could recuperate at leisure, putting handfuls of sugar lumps in your tea and savouring the company's Individual Fruit Pies as if they were the zenith of a pastry chef's art.

But however pleasant our runs were, they became increasingly clouded with a feeling of exclusion. Everywhere we went we were confronted with the presence of that fuller, grander world of organised cycling – the club. Long crocodiles of cyclists young and old, male and female, crossed our path wherever we went, tantalising us with the possibility of becoming part of a larger plan. There were boys of our own age in there, we had watched them romp and cheer with their elders as the clubs saluted each other. Our own timid efforts at the same thing were met with stony indifference. We would tag along with a trio of racing men, hoping to gain their attention by a demonstration of valour, but this brought little reward except more hostile stares. We were outsiders, pariahs, condemned by the very obviousness of our desire and the pitiful shortcomings of our production-line mounts. After so many rebuffs we would never have the nerve even to approach a club unless we sat astride a handbuilt lightweight. Our innocent little fetish had grown into a monster to haunt us.

Then Chris discovered a coterie of 'gen men' just a few doors down from his own; two brothers who were the centre of a circle of road-racers all belonging to a club called the Westwelve. Ron, the elder, had a Cinelli, and Harold another rarer Italian make that he had brought home from National Service in Trieste. There could be no doubt about their pedigree: they rode tubs and packed double clangers to a man. I ached to pay homage to the reality of this heady litany, so it wasn't long before we were out in Chris's back garden, peeping over the fence at these paragons as they lolled and sported like a pride of lions fat from good hunting.

Such brightly burning enthusiasts could not exist side by side for very long without attracting each other's attention. Chris's ardour was recognised and we were rewarded by an invitation to watch them race out at High Wycombe. Happy day. Would we get there, though? It was the furthest we had ever attempted.

Come the Sunday morning we set off into the unknown with a firm resolve and a full bottle of lemonade which only my saddlebag would accommodate.

We managed the run quite easily of course, and found the changing-rooms. This was our first exposure to that odd phenomenon, 'massed-start racing on public roads'. Mudguardless bikes were strewn everywhere, and figures in peculiar costume strode about with surprising composure given the eccentricity of their attire: shorts that verged on the indecent (a mixture of swimming togs and girls' gym-knickers); sagging jerseys weighed down at the back by a strange lumpy bustle. Then there was the Little-Lord-Fauntleroy primness below the knee: white ankle socks and dainty black pumps; and on their heads, a skimpy covering which crossed the knotted handkerchief with a jockey's cap to nobody's advantage. But there was another even more disturbing element. The unfamiliar expanses of flesh on view seemed curiously unused to such disclosure; there was a strange bruised baldness about it, like plucked chickens in a butcher's window.

We came upon Harold, our host, pumping up his racing tubulars on a grassy bank. His jersey was black with yellow-and-red rings and fitted him snugly; he was also reassuringly hairy. (It was quite some time before we made the unsettling discovery that the plucked-chicken effect was achieved with razor and shaving brush.) His head was crowned by a great dark-brown mop which fell about like windblown corn. He greeted us warmly but he was intent upon really hardening his tubs and our attention was drawn naturally to his bike. It was something special – a beautiful deep maroon with contrasting head. 'Julia', it said on the down-tube, a very un-italian ascription but one automatically revered. The lugs were rather plain, almost perfunctory in comparison to the more ornate English or French style which we were used to; the front forks seemed made for the track, they were so stocky, so curtly raked. Here was a robust uprightness, stripped for action, all its muscles showing. But then, for some reason, the handlebars veered towards us and there were these breathtaking amber-covered levers, as full and sturdy as the frame, the cables sweeping back in perfect unison to connect with an exquisite little caliper so finely drawn, so delicate that you were reminded of silverware – and indeed, it had its own hallmark sunk into the leading edge: 'Universal Milano'. All the accessories – the hubs, the gear levers, the wrinkled filigree of the Campagnolo *dérailleur* – were so finely wrought beside the columnar stateliness of the frame that the whole spoke of dynamism and refinement; of a culture which managed to blend strength with grace. This couldn't be a product of the burlesque land of pneumatic starlets and endless spaghetti, it must surely go back to that spirit which conquered the world – Imperial Rome. The man with the pump was subtly transformed into a classical legionary – his jersey a breastplate, the unmanageable mane of hair a plumed helmet; he was infantryman and gladiator both; a warrior athlete. In an instant he had won that special approbation which wells up so bountifully in a boy's heart: he had become a hero.

But where was he at the top of Marlow Hill? We had decamped in advance of the 'off' with the rest of the crowd to a vantage point on the outskirts of the town – a long, straight climb stretching away for nearly a mile below us. The ceremonial start was to be given outside the changing-rooms, but any racing would be 'neutralised' until the start proper at the top of our hill. We had heard this word 'neutralised' but failed to really grasp its meaning. It seemed to be linked in some impenetrable way to the sight of these 40-or-so riders packed tightly together and steadily eating up the road towards us. We had never seen such a phalanx of cyclists spread so far across the road. En masse and at a distance, they had ceased to be individuals but were transformed into a strange, rather threatening entity. They could have been the advance party of some sinister invading army, or even a monstrous caterpillar on a forest of metal legs with a knobbly, multicoloured back all seething and rippling – such was the incongruity of their presence on that peaceful Sunday morning in the foothills of the Chilterns.

The closer they approached, however, the more their strangeness receded; at short range their individuality was reconstituted. But there was no sign of Harold in that heaving throng. The mystery yawned in the wake of the last stragglers as they trickled out of sight. And then it was resolved – there he was, still down at the bottom, lost and struggling on his own. For a while it was like watching an ant hoist itself out of a mixing bowl, but then the man emerged. He was throwing himself at each succeeding ramp, out of the saddle, head bobbing urgently. Here was real racing at last, not the limp procession that we had just witnessed. An age seemed to elapse before he drew near.

'Come on, Harold,' we implored.

'Up, up, up,' shouted the gallery.

'Punctured on the line,' he gasped as he launched himself into the forlorn emptiness of the road ahead.

Teatime found us watching an official draw a finishing line across the road with a lump of natural chalk. We had had no guide to point out any other part of the course but the start and finish, so the burden of the afternoon still weighed upon us: would he make it?

Quite a crowd was gathering and each new arrival was greeted with ironic cheers. A rider in racing gear pedalled lackadaisically up to the line, dismounted and dived immediately in amongst the spectators, cutting short any such welcome. Then a shout went up to herald the arrival of the race. First there were two, then just one black figure thrusting down the middle of the road. The hair and desperation were unmistakable, it was Harold. And just as prompt as the recognition came the gagging, hissing cacophony of a body in violent throes. The intensity of his effort was frightening. He was all over the bike: stamping, heaving, wrenching; every last sinew coerced into flailing motion as he hurled himself towards the line. No challenger could live with this human locomotive, they fell back in dismay. With one final, convulsive kick he was home. He had won, our man had won. We swept after him with all the others. But even as we approached, the baleful news began to filter back.

'Pete Meredith went away up Stokenchurch. We never saw him again,' said the hero of the hour. That lone rider whose arrival had been so self-effacing was the real winner, he had tricked us with his casual victory.

But nothing could detract from the impressiveness of that sprint; man not machine had been the lesson of the day. There was more, much more, to aspire to than Nervex lugs or Stronglight cranks; we had been called away for ever from our narrow allegiance to the golden calf of good equipment.

2. Another World

By the early '90s my passion for the sport had cooled to the warm glow of a TV screen. I decided that I could not let another season pass without the luxury of Eurosport which shows all the single-day classics as well as the universally popular Tour de France 'live'. I had become an armchair aficionado. Years of watching borrowed videos and crawling round to perch awkwardly on other people's upholstery had primed me for complete control and unimpaired access. The pleasure was too intense to share.

Competitive cycling was made for TV, it provides the perfect vicarious experience. You are ushered into the previously undisclosed heart of the action; there, with the inimitable David Duffield talking it through, you get a pillion-ride with the gods. Those live transmissions carried me back to the days when I used to drool over the illustrated sporting press from France which was our only worthwhile contact with the great spectacles unfolding on the Continent. Such magazines were a revelation of another world, a vision scarcely credible set against the drab backcloth of the domestic scene. During the intervening years, however, technological advance had managed to telescope the whole process into moving pictures *en direct* – a triumph which was more than enough to re-ignite those teenage ardours.

A lot of the control I demanded was over the video recorder. What I wanted was an immaculate recording, as free as possible from those interminable ad-breaks; my dream was of a library of instantly retrievable pleasure. But I found, after a while, that

I was simply collecting the little black boxes; they lay there so long, some of them, that my son was pinching them to record over with his Kung-Fu dramas. It was one thing to draw the curtains and settle down for a live transmission and something else entirely to give up the same time for a re-run. The original dynamic was lost; even the most indolent of family men could not afford such indulgence.

Then I hit upon the scheme of actually riding while I viewed. What better way to finish off the evening's anti-ageing exercises than by catching a clip from the saddle?

'A home trainer,' my good friend Mario said, 'you can have mine. I couldn't stand it, too boring.' Thus after years of only desultory practice, I was back turning the pedals again on a regular basis – even if it was in my own front room.

What was tagged-on as a final flourish, however, became more and more time-consuming as I found that I couldn't mount the bike in the ordinary clothes I wore for the standard Canadian Air Force exercises, but must change into racing gear. After all, I had to put on cycling shoes, why not the full Lycra? Good form seemed to require it. Then there were the stretching exercises afterwards which were mandatory according to the experts – essential or an excuse for lingering before the video?

A competitive element soon made itself felt, as it was bound to, I suppose. Riding a bike is inherently competitive, you always want to go further and faster. I began to fix on the digital clock as intently as on the screen; the workouts became something of an evening time-trial. But however engrossing the session there was no mistaking the ersatz quality of the actual cycling; the home-trainer experience only vaguely approximated a real ride. The call of the open road sounded through every one of those dead pedal strokes.

Now this was dodgy territory, I had to be careful. The fitter I became the greater the risk, because one of the penalties I had incurred from a lifetime's cycling in and around the Smoke was a bad chest – specifically the sinister COAD, which spelled out means: Chronic Obstructive Airways Disease. Lung-searing efforts tended to have prolonged and nasty consequences. I had to pedal gingerly even behind closed doors. But the old fever was rising, there was no doubt. As soon as the cold weather abated, the bike and I would be nosing out into the smog for a spin around Richmond Park.

The course of my debility had seen many such resurrections and also many renunciations. The vehicle of so much delight had, on occasion, been an instrument of horror never to be touched or set eyes upon again. There was no mistaking, however, that my career had reached a bizarre pass with these regular pantomimes before the video screen. They gave rise to gentle misgivings about my state of mind, but past 50 you know that most of the world is as nutty as you are. What did begin to concern me, though, was the power of this so-called 'pastime'. Weren't similar absurdities being perpetrated all over the country? Wasn't a turbo trainer the in-vogue winter-training aid? Which begged the question: what possessed us all, what demented whim of human nature drew us to such a peculiar rapture?

This preoccupation took me through '93 and '94 without any resolution but a steady accumulation of miles both on and off the home trainer. Something of an answer came in early '95, however, with an article in *The Economist* surveying the coming season on the Continent under the headline: THE TOUGHEST SPORT? It was surprisingly perceptive and well informed, especially about the rigours of the early-season classics and the big Tours, but it was the final paragraphs that made me sit up. The anonymous writer quoted the results of a questionnaire completed by 100 French professionals in 1983:

> The poll was especially moving when the riders were asked why they entered the sport. Some 15 per cent said they had primarily sought glory, 12 per cent money and 3 per cent social mobility . . . Their overwhelming first choice? Nearly 40 per cent listed love of the sport as the main reason they turned professional; 30 per cent more listed it as their second choice.

One would have expected these tough road-men to be a bit more hard-headed, but they were obviously strong enough to admit the truth. It was love that made the wheels go round, even across the cobblestones in Paris–Roubaix – especially in Paris–Roubaix.

These findings were confirmed in a wonderfully downbeat picture of winter training Doncaster-style in an interview with John Tanner, the country's leading professional, later that year in *Cycling Weekly*. The local elite *grupetto* would be reduced in number that autumn because Wayne Randle was working in Halfords and Martin Maltby had acquired Don Valley Cycles. A bleak off-season was in prospect, but Tanner and Gary Speight would be getting in the miles for '96 in their usual dogged fashion and Tanner, the epitome of the gritty Yorkshireman, signed off with: 'You keep going because you like riding your bike . . . Nobody is doing it for money round here, it has to be love more than anything else.'

Love had bared its heart even in this most far-flung outpost, but love of what exactly? Just riding the bike, the thrill of racing or the companionship of like-minded souls? Did watching old videos from a home trainer qualify? Of course it did – love's bosom is notoriously ample. That was the trouble: as an explanation 'love' was too blanket, too all-embracing; it was ultimately unsatisfying. My hunch told me that there had to be something more. The heart was too large, too floppy – I wanted the lifeblood.

Then, just as the '96 season got under way, I turned my telly-watching into work experience. I persuaded Colin Coe, the editor of *Cycle News* (now sadly defunct) to take me on as TV critic; and in documenting the splendours and miseries of Eurosport I was forced to reconsider the attraction of the sport from a more specific angle. What was it in those blurred images that kept me, and thousands like me, glued to the screen? What was the essence of their popularity, their addictive pull?

A hitch occurred early on. Milan–San Remo, the first transmission of the year, failed to appear although it was listed.

I was, of course, beside myself – the first big showcase for my talents, the *Primavera*, festival of springtime. Quite apart from my new responsibilities, I wanted to bathe in that special Riviera light, watch it burn the picture off the screen. Instead we got one of those pre-recorded fillers showing yachts capsizing and skiers careering off piste – 'Bloopers' – which was exactly how we all must have felt. I stuck to my chair until the official announcement was posted, but then I was beached. The highlight of the day had been snuffed out. What could I do with myself and my disappointment? Immediately the box goes dead one's thoughts turn to the outside world and I remembered the morning's ride down to Shepherd's Bush Green to get the list of runners in *l'Equipe*. Everything had looked rosy then, even if it was on my shopping bike. I pulled the curtains and found that the sun was shining – not the Riviera dazzler – a paler English version, but the sun nonetheless. I would go out for a ride, launch the new season in proper style. As I took the bike down from the home trainer and replaced the front wheel, I was already leaving the let-down behind.

It was marvellous to be astride a 'live' bike once again. The machine was so sprightly that it seemed to dart forward on its own, like a fish from under a stone. It was in its element again, a wild thing let loose after a winter's captivity. The feeling overwhelmed me with its vividness, but also its familiarity – because this was how it always felt. There was always this poignant re-discovery which went back perhaps to that forgotten moment when you first learned the trick of it, when the wobbling and fear were left behind and you took off into freedom and wonder, borne by a motion which required so little effort and whose momentum simply fulfilled itself. The body was so harmoniously engaged that it seemed as if nature herself was imperceptibly lending a hand. This was what we loved on our racing machines, that primal 'feel' of mechanically enhanced motion, the sense of communion that it brought. I was more in touch with those bronzed supermen down on the Ligurian coast of Italy than ever I would have been in front of cable TV. Indeed, I was more in touch with myself. My disappointment had vanished under the first tyre tracks. All other considerations fell away in the free flow of movement. I had risen above every care; wings had been given me which I was calmly beating. That commonplace of science correspondents and television pundits about the bicycle being the most energy-efficient mode of travel had at last made sense. What else did those dry facts of mechanical engineering and physics mean but this transport of delight? I was living them, they had whisked me up and were carrying me along. Years of devoted ignorance fell away, I was alive to the reality with both heart and mind. In its humble and self-effacing way my old racing iron had always provided – and was providing now – another frame of reference, an access to another world. Just riding up the road was a transcendental experience. It was a re-enactment of that first kiss that seals a lifelong passion, the kiss which is offered and returned at will – the kiss of the pedals.

3. Mentors

Den Blissett had princely feet – a high instep which held the tongues of his *Grimpeur* shoes aloft like a banner. 'Ankling' was the received wisdom of those days – you dropped your heel on the downstroke and clawed the pedal round on the up. But Den never ankled; he favoured a firm rather than a supple ankle. It was all in the ball of the foot for him; there was something of the regimental slow march in the grave deliberation of his pedalling. Eventually I was able to afford my own *Grimpeurs* (seeking to emulate him) but my insteps wouldn't rise, my tongues lay doggo. When your feet come out from the heel as unrelieved as angle iron there is no way of disguising the fact – except, perhaps, by ankling.

Chris and I had been accepted into the Westwelve, and clubruns gave you ample opportunity to observe such fine points. The men you idolised simply because they rode good bikes and had raced were suddenly there, close at hand – you were sitting on their wheels. Each one quickly became a profile, a set of mannerisms, a style of movement which was quite distinct – and of course, you wanted to copy them, you wanted to slip inside their skins. The thought never occurred that you might be a set of mannerisms yourself, as distinct, as inviolable as theirs. No – such is the verve of youth that you were intent on improving upon nature, to make yourself up as an amalgam of all the best bits, quite unaware that this only made you into some scarecrow mixture of odd twitches and nods. It is called the confusion of growing up and is, of course, wholly necessary. Only by wearing yourself out with such antics do you fall back and simply be yourself. The men you imitate are aware to some degree of all this slavishness, but whether they pay any attention or not, simply by being there they become your mentors.

Den was the best rider in the club, a member of the West London Division team. He had a W.P. Newton frame with a pair of forks which were a work of art in themselves. He also had a full set of Campagnolo gears which were a real luxury in the mid-'50s. But Blissett never bothered too much with his machine; he rode the best available and that was it. A bike was only a bike as far as he was concerned. He did like riding it though; he rode everywhere. All he ever did besides racing was get plenty of miles in, he thrived on his stately pedalling.

In a club where great emphasis was placed on sprinting, he never contested a sprint. He hardly ever contested anything; it was a prolonged and careful discipline with him to save everything for the big occasion of an actual race. And he always wore mudguards – they were the emblem of this dedication. Even at the height of summer when everyone would simply leave them off – much as in the same way that you would lay aside trousers for shorts – Den would never discard his Bluemels. It was as if the spirited racehorse could only take on unbridled powers as long as it was firmly snaffled at all other times.

He was always good company, ready to laugh and joke, but he took no real part in the fancies of the more giddy members. He had little interest in the romance of the Continent. The furthest he would go in adulation of any kind was to speak reverently of national heroes like Bill Bradley or latterly of Ron Coe.

Yet he was the one who made the most progress in the sport. He represented West London in the Amateur Circuit of Britain and was picked for the Claud Butler team in the '55 Tour of Britain. He lined up with other luminaries as an aspirant or semi-professional with the option of going up to the paid ranks or being reinstated as an amateur at the end of the season. We didn't hear anything of him in the daily reports, but we all trooped up to Whitestone Ponds in Hampstead to see the finish of the final stage. Doug Booker of Viking romped away to victory from the Hercules man, Dennis Talbot; followed after a gap by Brian Haskell and then, wonder of wonders, came Blissett on his new yellow bike. He looked tremendous. A fortnight's wind and rain had done marvels for his already swarthy complexion, he was tanned nut-brown – and his legs were shaved. This was a new, slick version of our old club-mate.

'Come on, Blissett,' said one of the company drily (the rest of us were completely agog) and he looked up from his labours to crease his face into a weak smile.

The next weekend he was back in an amateur bunch, a 100 miles around the Chobham circuit. From the first lap he put his stamp on the race, leading the bunch down the hill by the changing-rooms. Hair parted down the middle, turning a big gear easily, his slightly hooked nose cleaving the wind – he made the rest look like a raggle-taggle.

Halfway through, a break went and we had a few men up there, but Den was in command. Lap after lap the numbers diminished until at the bell there were only two left: Blissett and some reinstated ex-Hercules rider. Would our man get his revenge for the previous week? The race had been a classic war of attrition and Den looked the stronger of the two. The final skirmishes were lost around the back, on the climbs; we had to wait it out on the finishing stretch. But sure enough, after an eternity, the familiar black silhouette hove into view, and he stormed across the line putting minutes onto his erstwhile companion. It was a stirring demonstration of the class and fitness he had honed to perfection in the national tour. But once changed, he put his mudguards back on, fastened trouser clips to the brown serge trousers which were another trademark, and rode home with us.

If Blissett was a swarthy Mediterranean without the hot blood, then Ron Chitty was a pale Anglo-Saxon with a latin temperament. There was a flair about Ron; a swashbuckling zest which was irresistible and it was reflected in the manner of his riding. He swivelled from side to side with each pedal thrust in the manner of the day, but with him it was widened and stretched so that his shoulders were all the time bobbing and weaving a loose figure of eight into the headwind. It was completely natural and unforced, a way of channelling the abundant steam that flowed through him. He loved throwing himself – and the bike – about. His movements were always large and sweeping – he loved gesture. He spoke very eloquently with his body, though he loved words too. He would seize upon some prize example and relish the sound of it, mime its every syllable – *animateur* was one of his favourites. He had a full repertoire of gesticulations for all the mad conjugations he could think up. When it came to those French magazines he would force the images off the page with improvisations and elaborations carved from the air, blowing them up until they burst.

The bike was like a trapeze to him, he could almost swing from it. He could do all the tricks: stand on the saddle, steer with his foot, put his nose on the front wheel. He was a master of descending; he could perch straight-legged and still over the bars and let the bike plummet down a hill like nobody else. Or he could shrivel up so tightly in your slipstream that he would be able to breeze by in the last few yards. There was nothing he liked better than to crash off across country, turning the run into some hare-brained scramble which skirted disaster and ended up in helpless laughter. We went cyclo-cross training in Richmond Park once. We were actually rough-stuffing it with the deer when suddenly we were rounded up by a keeper on a huge horse. Ron stood his ground and offered to box the man's silly bowler from his head if he cared to dismount. The keeper was dumbstruck, and we were able to retreat in good order, grinning like schoolboys.

A lot of his élan had been shaped by the experience of National Service in Egypt; he had obviously enjoyed himself scampering about the desert. His language was peppered with army expressions; much play was made of the 'pit', for instance, and the joys of being in it. His favourite item of clothing was another inheritance from this era, a pair of lightweight tan trousers which he called his 'KDs'.

His first senior win in a road race came out of the blue – literally. It was on the Ashdown circuit, on a beautiful early summer afternoon with a major part of the sky spread out before us. The bunch presented itself intact on the final stretch of a long climb; they were all struggling. Suddenly a black figure flailing about like an eel whipped around the offside and was across the line in a few more convulsive kicks. Over in a flash and won – it was a typical Chitty effort, and much moaned about subsequently by rivals whom he had caught napping.

The ride home was a triumphal progress. Ron, like a victorious general flanked by his cohorts, his beloved KDs rolled up and flapping about the legs that had done such sterling work, waved ostentatiously to every other club we met on the way.

Harold ('Bo' to the club) was way ahead of his time, he extolled the virtues of women and womanhood long before they started piping up for themselves. Girlfriends – if they existed – were never usually mentioned; they didn't fit in with the ideal of monastic dedication which was the prevailing orthodoxy. But Bo had a girl – not only that, he flaunted her. Immediately his foot hit the kerb after a long day pushing the pedals (all our rides began and ended at his house) he would shout, 'Hildaaaaah . . . ' until a top window of the flats opposite flew open and there would be his Juliet.

'Put the kettle on,' he'd say.

Theirs was the balcony scene of Emlyn Road. Mind you, he had been a free-thinker from an early age, he even called his parents by their first names: Maude and Sid.

He was the hub of our little wheel: everyone's friend and confidant, the leader, the father figure, the guru. He was extremely practical, down-to-earth and tirelessly energetic; but he was also a visionary and that gave him his real hold over us. He could speak knowingly of the respect and status afforded to racing men on the Continent – he had actually been there and experienced it for himself during his National Service in Trieste. From that knowledge to a ready identification with the great aces was an easy step – one that he encouraged in others. England was all right as a training ground, but one's sights had to be set on the real world which was across the Channel. He was a prophet; a voice crying in the wilderness of our small corner of insular, post-war Britain, and we became his faithful disciples. He would lead us to the Promised Land or at least inspire us to go for ourselves.

In the autumn of the first year I knew him, he decided that he had never really been well-served by the beautiful Julia he had brought home from Italy, that what he needed was a frame built very precisely to his own specifications. The manner and matter of these specifications took on the import of an alchemical prescription during the months that followed. It was endlessly elaborated and discussed and he swept us all up into the formulation of the spell. What we were forging was not just a new frame, but a talisman, some magic vehicle which would transform the rider; set him on his way towards the realisation of his dreams – all our dreams.

The new season dawned and the first trials proved satisfactory, but the real acid test would, of course, be a race. So we all trundled over to the Essex Grand Prix, as we called it.

When we got there it was to learn the disconcerting news that a team of Belgians had been included in the field. Belgians in sleepy, ribbon-developed Essex – it seemed hardly credible. Even as spectators we were put on our mettle. There was something threatening about them, these shadowy gremlins from the hinterland of Roubaix, the Hell of the North. They raced around the houses and their monarch was Rik Van Steenbergen – 'King of the Sixes'. His name alone announced his kingship as far as we were concerned and it was much bandied about; but the thought of his subjects running amok struck fear into the heart. We waited with bated breath along the Southend arterial. And we were not disappointed.

A small, hectic blob of motion appeared in the distance. It rapidly became a surging articulation of shoulders, arms, legs, hissing and heaving all over a bike which remained rock-steady and dead on course. He was obviously a Belgian, just from the lack of anything approaching style – but what energy and commitment. *Whoosh* – he hit the line with the momentum of the Coronation Scot – and left a great vacuum behind him. Minutes later Ted Gerrard won the bunch sprint, but no one else really mattered.

We had seen one of the great finishers: Arthur De Cabooter, a man who was eventually to win the Tour of Flanders, and spread himself across the covers of the French magazines in the *style rageur* we had just been witness to. His power was magnetic; we rushed to join the crowd around him. The manager was a big, fat man in a greasy, fawn mac and a maize paper Gauloise stuck to his lip. Another of his riders came in with the bunch, he was dark and wolfish and wore a little silk scarf knotted around his neck. All of them were gulping and gobbling their strange tongue to each other. They were like Romanies; Martians even – unfathomable. We turned to one of their bikes hoping to find a key. The finish on the frame was pure psychedelia long before the term was even thought of. A peculiar deep purple crackle swept forward from the rear triangle to fade into pale yellow along the crossbar and up from the bottom-bracket. 'Plume Vainqueur' proclaimed the heavy gold letters on the down tube. This garishness coupled with some odd workaday details like rubber cotton reels around the brake levers suggested a trick cyclist, something from a funfair or the circus. The mystery and the awe deepened; these blokes were wall-of-death riders, dare-devils from another universe.

Bo, too, was full of the Belgians: 'That blonde one was straight up the kerb when he attacked, dived between two old ladies going to church, he did. I've never seen anything like it.'

The fabled realm had come to life: they did actually race on the pavements in Belgium, they were hell-for-leather merchants.

'He's been riding the boards all winter. Those blokes never stop racing. I'll bet they've just finished a six-day.' What a country it seemed suddenly, continuous racing indoor and out, jumping up on the kerb, hammering around the boards – a bike rider's paradise. The new frame, everything else was forgotten; we looked at the strange trio with all-devouring eyes. They were messengers from afar, heralds of a more abundant life.

At the end of the season, Bo made the startling announcement that he and Ron were forsaking the road and devoting themselves to the track. There were more openings abroad for track-men, he explained; the track scene was an unexploited back door which they would use to full advantage. Whatever reservations the other club members may have entertained, Chris and I were so completely in thrall to the glowing perspectives he had previously held before us that we could find no voice or reason to question these new horizons, much less divine that our brush with the Belgians had sparked it all. Any sense of betrayal or resentment was quickly smoothed away by the weekly ritual of the clubrun. It was business as usual, but with a fixed wheel.

If nothing seemed to have changed for us there was still an almost imperceptible shift away from our leading mentor. Unconsciously we felt so secure in our own golden future that this reshuffle made little impact except to separate the generations. We understood intuitively that any pioneering work by our elders could only pave the way for us; in our heart of hearts we enjoyed the supreme, untried certainty of youth. Looking down from the ramparts of our dreams, there was no question but that the meek would inherit the earth.

4. The Frame of Reference

I'm still riding my first 'new' racing frame which I bought on the never-never in 1958; it rejoices in the imprimatur of one Fred Dean (anonymously now, since the primitive red stencil on the top tube disappeared under a respray decades ago). Fred was a loyal Claud Butler manager – a name of some repute in those days – until the grand old man went bust, at which point Fred set up on his own. In order to give his name some currency he fielded a trade team – well, hardly a team, a few blokes here and there – eventually backing the legendary 'Mighty Atom', Dave Bedwell, in his declining years. Fred's favourite colour and brand image was a rich, Van Gogh yellow; a real South-of-France hue which immediately won my teenage heart. The last Claud Butler team in the 1955 Tour of Britain with Jock Andrews, Johnny Morris, Jim Higgins, Ian Barnet – and my club-mate Den Blissett – had ridden bikes of a similar shade, so I was primed. In the background, of course, was the Sun King himself, Louison Bobet, garlanding the yellow of his new namesake mount (courtesy of Mercier) with rainbow stripes for his World Champion's season of the same year. Yellow has always been one of the emblematic colours of cycling, look no further than the *maillot jaune*.

This object of so much desire was originally built for 'Gino' Goddard who was still racing until just recently. I've seen him out at events but have yet to collar him for the full story of his flirtation with the paid ranks – and why he remained pure, thus allowing his frame to fall my way for a discounted twenty-two quid.

There seems to be a remarkable stamina in that whole generation which is reflected in the strength of the veteran scene overall. Like my bike they go on and on. It's still a bit small and I'm too far behind the bottom bracket, but I'm unlikely to get another until it gives up the ghost. This is blithe talk perhaps, since there is every indication that it will see me out. Whatever sentimental fancies I may entertain, it's hard to avoid the fact that I am just a fleeting episode in its low-key mineral existence. The flurry of life I bring to it on occasion may add no spark to its essentially stillborn condition – the very lifelessness which guarantees longevity. The thing I most cherish thereby becomes a reproof to my human lifespan; a memento mori all the more telling for having been party so long to my own lifecycle.

While we're on last things, I might mention that I once nearly killed for it. At the time I was living in a block of flats with a single outside staircase and I used to leave my bike chained to a dustbin on the landing. One Sunday afternoon I heard a strange noise outside and upon opening the front door found some wretch applying a tourniquet to the lock. He had pushed the dustbin over so that my way was blocked and he immediately took off. I was so taken aback that he was already two flights down before I even thought of giving chase. I knew though that he only had two choices out of the entrance and the porthole beside me overlooked one of them. I grabbed a full black bag from out of the dustbin and waited for him to show. It was a fifty-fifty chance; the only problem being how far out to hurl my counter-strike. He duly emerged and I launched my missile – only then registering the presence of the tubular steel base of an old office chair atop the rubbish. From three flights up it would surely cave his skull. My heart was in my mouth for the eternity that the bag took to drop with a frightening jangle. How glad I was to see him still scarpering away; for a few moments I had felt the damp chill of a condemned cell.

Bikes are like birds, they never seem to die. There are no bike graveyards, no cycle crematoria, no two-wheeled knacker's yards to my knowledge. True there are the odd skeletons chained to railings, picked almost clean by various predators; a few steadily rusting hulks tucked away in sheds and down alleys, but compared to the other wheeling flocks and swarms in lively motion this evidence is at best inconclusive. What happens to the long and the short and the tall *not* sold at police auctions? No doubt they are shipped off to the Third World like the lorry-loads of stolen lightweights that regularly leave these shores for the Continent. The bicycle is eminently recyclable; there is something eternal about a diamond frame and a spinning wheel.

Back in the early '80s, I found the perfect frame – 23", Nervex pro lugs, Campag ends, obviously a handbuilt lightweight toshed-up with a coat of black paint – abandoned in the gutter after the departure of a council skip. Unfortunately it was during one of those periods when I despaired of ever straddling a bike again. I kept it in the attic until a fit of generosity prompted me to give it to a friend. He had it built up and still rides it when I twist his arm. In the meantime he's gone over to the other side – to the gas pipe specials that allow you to ride off the kerb without feeling a thing: great sport – while I'm left with my dear old Dutch. It's one of those relationships similar to a longstanding marriage: a low glow full of cosy familiarity. There are moments when I catch sight of her in the hall, though, and my heart does a scuba dive – the line of her, the curves: a beauty still.

We love bikes because they are the physical representation of the subtle pleasure that we derive from them. They act upon us both as a symbol and as the means of fulfilment; we adore them but we also want to possess them. The love they inspire is as carnal as it is spiritual – much the same as we feel for the opposite sex. I know plurocrats who treat themselves to a new metallic mistress every third season or so, and others who keep a harem in the garage.

At the heart of a bike is that engineering marvel, the spoked wheel. Every other component tries to match its spare purity. Spin a wheel and the spokes disappear; the rim turns as if independently, but is always held by those invisible stays. That apparent void not only bears the weight of the rest of the fragile construction but also supports a bulky human being as well. It is this perceptual conundrum which creates the airy insubstantiality of the whole; the everyday hyper-reality that casts the spell of poetry over its passage.

My equipment-fetishist days were short-lived, nipped in the bud as it were. I got into a school which went to the other extreme: the rag and bone merchants. Most of our stuff was old or second-hand anyway so we made a virtue out of necessity. We would ride anything that came along, and the cheaper the better. (Flashback to Derek Moss, a fond and tragic memory. One of the leaders of the school, he even had the furtive looks of a gypsy – winning tens at Paddington track on Pirelli Gran Premios, a heavy road tub of the day. He died on his bike in a motor accident on the A40 some years ago.) I did my racing on Benelux gears, the British Simplex; and as with the original, you could adjust the rear arm with a well-placed wrench and a bit of torque. There was something defiant in such a stance – and a laziness too, of course – you had to ride harder. It was an implicit challenge to yourself and to the spoke polishers. Indeed, I still find it hard to clean my bike – all it usually gets is a quick brush-down before the off – and yet . . . and yet I treasure it.

No doubt I would treasure a Colnago C40 or a Lemond Galibier, but those are just lottery dreams. My old Fred Dean precisely matches my requirements and my aspirations; we are a reflection of each other. We share a certain careworn shabbiness. We could both do with a thorough overhaul, a face lift, a bit of structural surgery perhaps, some sort of transplant. But the real covenant which unites us has nothing to do with appearances. What we do together is what counts, that marvellous complicity which puts the clock back to zero and releases us into the joy of the here and now.

A lightweight cycle is such an evolved mechanism that it demands the same level of perfection in the rider. Speed and aerodynamics require a crouch which imitates the angularity of the frame: the crook of the arm, the flexing of the knee, the articulation of back and thighs all mimic the bike's geometry. Tour de France competitors work hard to reduce their body fat before the race and become so lean during the three weeks of battle that they begin to resemble the stark purity of their mounts. Bjarne Riis was a striking contemporary example. Felice Gimondi in his prime was also seen to pass through that tempering flame. Fausto Coppi always seemed to be an elongation of his Bianchi. Eddy Merckx though was an exception; he never approached that almost mechanical unity, he was never 'part of the bike' as was said of Jacques Anquetil. He tended to be all over it, fighting it, driven and possessed by that phenomenal energy.

The professional scene is the crucible from which all the moulds are cast. Paradoxically, however, the bike is of much less importance to the top-level pro than it is to the ordinary enthusiast simply because all the tools of his trade are the concern of the sponsor. There are a host of models at his disposal. He doesn't even have to take care of them, the mechanic does that. If something goes wrong during a race he dumps the offending article and grabs another. When he moves on to a different team he is automatically issued with a whole stable of made-to-measure replicas in his new colours. Even when he retires, he discards the reminders of his glory days. Eddy Merckx has long since forsaken his Molteni orange Colnago, as Roger De Vlaeminck has done with his Gios; their status is such that they have achieved a lifetime's access to an appropriate bike.

The stars transcend their vehicles; once the race is finished, the bike is wheeled away into the wings. The protocol of victory demands that the rider alone steps up to the podium. I remember seeing the finish of the '74 Tour on the old *Municipale* track in Paris. While Merckx and co. were enjoying the spotlight, the remains of the *peloton* were still milling around in the track centre – on their bikes. It was as if they could not dismount, that 2,000 miles had fused them to their saddles. The team-men, the *domestiques*, all the other ranks really do become part of the bike; they seem to be tied to their two-wheeled treadmills like laboratory animals, until success brings release.

For the majority, though, that deliverance never comes; they hang up their wheels in much the same anonymity as they had when they first squeezed home their quick releases. So the pitched battle of the *peloton* rages first with the effort to rise above the ruck and then to transcend the bike itself. The real measure of a big name is the extent to which he no longer depends on the humble conveyance that first brought him to notice. At the higher reaches of fame the champion has so transfixed the competition that when the decisive moment comes they are almost waiting for him to take off, such is his power of assertion, a power which goes well beyond the business of urging the machine forward. Legendary figures, of course, have always been borne along on the magic swell of universal acclaim; their feet need hardly touch the pedals. Coppi's legs turn forever in the lubricant of wonder, levelling out every gradient and widening gaps irredeemably. He is pure inspiration soaring skywards, no longer pushing the bike but clutching it between his talons.

When Enzo Ferrari, the famous racing-car builder said that: 'Between man and machine there exists a perfect equation, fifty per cent machine and fifty per cent man,' he spoke more truly perhaps of the racing bike. You get on it, pedal up the road and immediately feel the silky, effortless motion that it provides. But go a few miles, confront a hill maybe, and the bike begins to call on your fifty per cent. Are you fit and strong enough to do it justice? That transport of delight can become something of a calvary. You have to balance the equation, you have to live up to those sublime mechanics. This is why so many expensive purchases are quickly discarded by novices young and old; the responsibility is too heavy, the self-confrontation too searching. But of course if you do rise to the challenge, if you are prepared to undergo the training that your mount demands, your enjoyment will be fuller and more satisfying than a mere joyride. You can become equal partners in a wonderfully fulfilling discovery of both body and mind. You can touch upon a sense of life which is freer and more abundant; a transformation of consciousness which inspires cultivation. Such is the secret that all keen cyclists share and generally keep to themselves – for it cannot be taught, only picked up for oneself like the initial skill of riding. A tacit reverence exists comparable to those religions for whom the name of the deity is so sacred that it is never uttered aloud. The bike itself remains its own most compelling evangelist. All the great celebrations of the cycling calendar from the Tour de France downwards are a demonstration of its liberating truth. The only outward sign is that passed between enthusiasts when they are out riding: they will acknowledge each other with a discreet nod or wave, a recognition of the esoteric bond which unites otherwise perfect strangers.

This is why the bike is so important to the average enthusiast. It is his charger, his suit of armour and his coat of arms; it proclaims that he has sworn himself to the quest for the mystic grail; it is his sword of honour which allows him to defer to and receive back the deference of his peers. In the saddle he is a DIY knight of the road who may pedal in solitude, but is never alone.

Of course, the other side of the coin is that you are the bike that you ride. In contrast to the production-line sameness of the professional's issue, the average enthusiast's bike is the sum of carefully weighed decisions. It is thought out and pieced together and therefore becomes a very personal statement. Whether ostentatious or self-effacing, everything about you is on display. Your gimlet-eyed colleagues are able to place you very precisely in the hierarchy at a single glance. Scant regard will be paid to your person; the real message is in the pedigree of your frame, the setting of your brake levers and a hundred other fine details that they will pick up almost by radar. The scrutiny is as intense as it is well practised, so you return the favour with matching sharpness, thus fulfilling your part of this 'highway code'. You will come across them wherever you go. They are out there waiting and wondering just like you – the uneasy corps of the self-made Round Table.

There are knights of another order on the far side of the road these days, although they might reject any such title, or even the concept of knighthood. They are more like a peasant revolt, for their implements come straight from the farmyard. Like dwarf shire horses bred for squatness and bulk, their mounts are a troll-like deformation of our graceful pure-breds. This overt ugliness is their badge of honour, an article of faith. They are a kind of protestant sect which has risen with Lutheran rectitude to challenge the established Church. They preach a return to the land, to bridle paths and ridgeways in the absence of mountains. 'Rough Stuff', we used to call it; indeed, we have a competitive discipline which provides for this very tendency called Cyclo-Cross that still has a following. But these upstarts have tried to usurp all our prerogatives which is rather galling since they seem to make little effort to practice what they preach. Are they to be found in the fabled 'off-road'? Hardly at all. They're out parading the highways with their grotesque parody of true cycling. We have bided our time and waited for all the Billy Graham-ism to die down, but the holy rollers have increased and multiplied – even worse, the majority of the lay population has been converted. As is usual in religious matters, big money has taken a hand; even the lily-livered press has kowtowed. A kind of Reformation has swept the cycling world and we're now on the verge of being put out to grass ourselves. We're under enough threat from motor traffic, and police restrictions on our regular Sunday services of time-trials and road racing, without these heretics tub-thumping about a return to the primeval slime. We are a house divided and nowhere is this division more keenly felt than out on the road.

What are they doing there at all, the hypocrites, why aren't they down in the woods at least? This is the big contradiction of the mountain-bike phenomenon.

Previous fads like the Chopper and BMX weren't taken up by adults, but the mountain bike has seemingly tapped some deep-seated urban *nostalgie de la boue* – literally. ('If my knotty tyres make it feel like I'm riding through mud then I must be in the country' – or some similar mental/emotional back-flip.) Choosing to drive a tractor instead of a car might at least be justifiable as a dotty indulgence – after all, the engine is there to do the work – but *pedalling* the thing? For pleasure? All right, people are back on bikes again, but only in a travesty of the real experience.

The late Emil Zatopek, a famous Czech athlete (three gold medals in the 1952 Olympics, a feat never equalled in long-distance running) used to train in hob-nailed boots regularly, but not continuously. In my experience the mountain bike is the equivalent of wearing hob-nailed boots – all the time. It is an aberration, a mixture of fashion delirium and puritan backlash. How else can one explain the fact that they are almost overwhelmingly confined to big cities? Do they really summon up the rural idyll in the midst of unredeemed concrete? The same might be asked of those four-wheel-drive landcruisers, the state coaches of the grossly rich, they're pure delusion too. But are the showrooms chock-full of them almost to the exclusion of anything else? That's what has happened to the cycle trade; even run-of-the-mill commuters are now complaining that there's nothing decent to ride. We are taking to the hills in droves, it would appear – but our inclinations are still smoothly metalled. You can soak up the potholes on your MTB, but who fancies riding out to do some real mud plugging? It's hard graft churning those balloon tyres, and that is perhaps the secret of their appeal. You've got to get all that ballast moving at a fair lick or else you begin to grind to a halt. What you buy is an intensive workout, there's no freewheeling. It's 'going for the burn' the whole way; the gym on wheels, all sweat and no play – puritan fundamentalism set in a California dreamland. Broad shoulders, shaven skulls, tree-trunk legs and Timberland boots – it's country cousin meets Roundhead chic. They're good, those boys, as they punch by in a buzz of scorching rubber – worthy heirs to Zatopek's Stalinist training regimes. We might well be producing a generation of superchampions – the swine certainly have a tendency to muscle by me in the park.

For all that, we must be grateful for the mountain bike; at least millions are still pushing the pedals round – albeit in a degraded fashion, but pedalling nonetheless. The doctrinal issue has subsided – as has the coverage of MTB sport, it has to be said. The whole flare-up appears to be in its dying-embers stage; even dedicated racing men often keep a spare cart-horse in the garage for those relaxing off-season capers in the mud. MTBs might have had a dire effect on lightweight and utilitarian design, bringing in brutality where refinement once reigned, but there is no doubt that they were the salvation of the cycle trade. What the whole phenomenon demonstrates, though, is the enduring soundness of the basic principle which allows the bicycle to adapt and re-invent itself for every age.

5. Sepia Magic

It wasn't love at first sight with the 'continental magazines', as they were called. Sometimes the adventurous would refer to 'but clubs' or 'mirror sprints', but only the O level prig that I was ever attempted the correct pronunciations: *But-et-Club* and *Miroir-Sprint* which are unwieldy even on French lips and sound like baby-talk to our native ears.

A lightning-bolt of recognition it was not. I saw this sickly brown thing lying on the café table like an oversized Victorian postcard, and I wasn't taken. That sepia tone, which I would grow to love, reminded me then of old family photographs with bygone relatives staring out from a kind of congealed death. Perhaps I flicked through it, was impressed by the large pictures and the novelty of a magazine written in French, but all I can remember is my initial distaste. One of the more intellectual club members would have brought it along. There was a coterie of office types – what today would be called 'young professionals' – with whom I never really got on, probably because I was something of a strung-up teenager. Later, I would convert the pale gelatine of first impressions into the rich milk chocolate of wholesale adoration, but nothing of the glamour and excitement of a highly developed popular culture from across the Channel seems to have penetrated immediately.

Only when I befriended Arthur George James (otherwise known as 'Specs', one of the non-racing members); and discovered his cache of Tour de France souvenir issues which were printed in black and white, did the love affair spark into life. Once hooked, I used to drop in on him, as if casually, just to catch another glimpse of these treasures. He lived a strange, embattled existence confined to the first floor of his father's semi. The old boy – a rather dumpy, unimpressive figure compared to his strapping son – had remarried, and his new bride, herself a large, imposing woman, would only tolerate the grown-up stepson under the same roof, it seemed, as long as he kept himself very much to himself. Visits were always a bit daunting for fear of crossing this battleaxe. The usual procedure was to shout up to the window rather than suffer the frosty reception that might ensue from ringing the doorbell. But it was all worthwhile once you were in Specs' stronghold with its flip-top stool housing the golden folios.

The covers were resplendent in retouched colour which was an unusual luxury for the day, and inside the year's odyssey unfolded in soft, grey tones rather than stark black and white. In 1951 there was the incredible Swiss smoothie, Hugo Koblet, combing his hair before the finishes and wearing his goggles round his upper arm. He had the looks of a matinee idol and class to match; there was a whole section devoted to his epic lone break when he held off the crème de la crème of the day along sun-drenched *Routes Nationales* for 150 kilometres. Then came the equally imperial Coppi of '52, perched on his Bianchi like some improbable flamingo, his spindly legs turning the pedals irresistibly. 1953 saw the long-awaited accession of Louison Bobet, the French pin-up; he repeated the feat again in '54, setting the stage for the unprecedented triumph of '55: a hat-trick. These lavish pictorial records (only a few words of the text proved decipherable) were so rich, so spell-binding that each dip provided a banquet of thrills, illuminations; yearning desires for bikes, for jerseys – but above all else for the magazines themselves. Specs, however, had made it clear from the beginning that the precious tomes could never leave the premises.

The feeling grew from each perusal that I had in my hands

enough excitement and delight to swallow hours of entranced study. Here was the Book of Revelation, a prospectus for the Promised Land. Here was evidence that our poor, hangdog little sport was capable of rising to heights of epic grandeur. These riders were national heroes, the whole country turned out to watch them pass by; the finish on its own was comparable to a Cup Final. In France it was obvious that anyone who rode a bike was potentially a star sportsman, not condemned to the scathing disregard one felt in this country. The Tour was a celebration on a national scale of the values that came up to me through my legs from the pedals – values which I could only share with a small band of fellow enthusiasts, itself a tiny cell in a rather diffuse minority movement. Yet here was splendid proof that those very same values held good for a whole country, even the majority of a Continent. Over there a racing bike was a symbol of the highest athletic prowess.

What overwhelmed me was the size and vividness of the images, the faces jubilant in victory or downcast by defeat, the stricken, bloodstained crash victims, the thickets of spectators by the roadsides, the sweep of a whole *peloton* in full flight, the great panoramas of countryside and architectural showpieces, and, of course, the majestic backcloth of the high mountains. I fell in love with the land, the language, everything to do with such a great-hearted people. The title of one of the accompanying texts lodged in my mind: *La Toison d'Or*. It seemed to sum up the experience of turning those pages, of soaking up picture after picture until you were drunk with the abundance and the intoxicating message which they held out: that there was within reach a paradise of cycling to which you were a natural heir; that you were, for the moment, an exile who could only share in its bounty at a remove – but one day you might be able to go there and to take up your inheritance.

I made no effort to look up the words, they were more important than mere knowledge; they became the secret formula for that whole condition of exaltation which would inform and enrich the next few years. Eventually, by intuition or accident, I discovered that they meant: 'The Golden Fleece', a reference which combined classical myth with the yellow jersey – precisely the high-flown aspiration and quest which I felt I had embarked upon.

My aversion to sepia was thus swept away under the spell cast by good old black and white, but there was another 'colour shock' in store. I subsequently discovered the same magazine again only in a rich indigo. Apparently each week brought a change of ink for both titles, so that the colours alternated in tandem. But there was yet another twist: an alternation in the depth of the tone. The sepia would vary between a light milk chocolate and a dark plain chocolate, and the indigo – the colour of jeans – exploited a full range of possible blues from the heavy saturation of first purchase to the faded azure of the nth wash.

Your way of seeing was changed for ever by those brown and blue inks; you began to view yourself through those monochrome filters, because it was *you* in there in those lustrous stills. The riders may have been dressed up in fancy attire, but those grimaces, those hunched shoulders, those muscle striations crying out in pain, even the euphoric grins – were nothing other than your own; you knew exactly how it felt. In fact, it was your little life writ large there upon the page. The response went beyond identification. It was colonisation by right. Your imagination had found a new mode of expression and burst forth into realms vast beyond all expectation. You were affirmed and legitimised by those images, and, to cap it all – glorified. From then on every act, every nuance of movement on the bike could be seen in the light of that warm blue or brown; everyone was acting up for the unseen camera, we played our parts with gusto in a generally condoned flight of fancy.

Along the way I had picked up another friend through courting his sister. The courtship was short-lived but Blaise, who was a couple of years older, revealed a more solid basis for affection. He had recently been given a new bike which he was going to ride to Ireland. I too went to Ireland that year, but without my bike. I was off it in fact for something like six weeks. When I returned, Blaise suggested a ride together and he completely thrashed me coming back from the airport. This was a bitter blow, a newcomer showing me the way home, whatever the disparity in recent miles. Chris and I plotted to work him over on the Guildford road but to no avail, he was always that little bit stronger on the climbs and in sprints. Nevertheless (or maybe as a result) he became a regular companion and a firm friend. We eventually introduced him to the club, though I think we held back a bit because of his cut-glass accent and strange name, but he quickly established himself.

Blaise was instrumental in finding the source of the magazines because of his familiarity with the West End. He led me to Moroni's shop in Old Compton Street where they could be bought. In fact there were several newsagents along that road where you could pick up French and also Italian magazines. It was a treasure trove because most of the stock was on racks outside the shops, just inviting inspection. There was a different atmosphere up there, business was more relaxed. The usual griping, hawk-eyed 'if-you-don't-want-the-goods-don't-muck-'em-about' cockney gave way to a benign patriarch holding court in his little emporium, usually speaking Italian – it was almost like being abroad.

In those days none of the national dailies carried any news of the Tour; foreign magazines were the only source of really up-to-date information because they came out twice weekly. I well remember the Saturday morning Blaise and I went up to Moroni's to get the first report of the '56 Tour, and found Brian Robinson on the cover. He had managed a good third place to Darrigade on the first stage and there he was dancing on his pedals at the head of the world's greatest cycle race. As part of the ground-breaking Hercules team the year before, he had finished a creditable 29th, the first Englishman to complete the distance, but he had hardly got a mention. Now he had arrived with a bang. We felt that something momentous had occurred – for Brian and for us. The message was as clear as his picture: he had forced his way into the pantheon of azure and gold, he had honked his way up among the Greats. If he could do it then there was a chance that we too might leave our mark in that revered ink.

From that moment on the magazines became our news from the Front, the necessary dispatches to the civilian sympathisers and future combatants. They no longer enshrined a fervent hope, they documented a living possibility. We became even more besotted by the parlance and usages of that special world we had fleshed out from our studies. All those *primes* that we fought out on hilltops in Buckinghamshire were for a *Grand Prix de la Montagne* of some endless epic held in the imagination of the bunch who disputed them. Every town sign became a mocked-up *arrivée*, every café stop a *contrôle de ravitaillement*. We were all classified as *rouleurs, grimpeurs* or generally *animateurs*; sometimes a great ace, sometimes a *domestique* – it was like an incantation, a prayer.

We became more continental than the continentals; we shouted and gesticulated in this bastard language, we threw our bikes about more extravagantly, we elbowed and leant and grabbed jerseys. We had already moved into a halfway house between our own familiar roads and the vistas of the hallowed ground across the Channel; we were on our way.

Was it an accident that both blue and brown had a religious connotation: one the symbol of heaven and the other of self-sacrifice – the garb most noticeably worn by the followers of St Francis? Was it Robinson's serene countenance, even in the heat of battle, that made us aspire to a kind of saintliness?

Whatever the case there was a religious devotion to our efforts; we donned our habits even if they were only mental attitudes; we endeavoured to live like monks. Hard riding and clean living were the order of the day. Non-bike-riding women were, of course, a very dangerous distraction. Although Bo flaunted Hilda, his heresy only served to galvanise the resolve of the righteous. If you weren't out forming an echelon up the Great West Road or really up West getting the latest bulletin from Moroni's, then you congregated, like early Christians in the catacombs, in small, cramped places of refuge and worship – cycle shops.

There you would mill about among devotional objects (frames, sprints, chainwheels); or among vestments (racing jerseys in various denominational colours, massed-start caps, and those long woollen shorts in ecclesiastical black); or if the season was propitious, touch sacred relics ('Jock Andrews's actual bike as ridden in the Tour of Britain').

And all around there would be holy pictures; for it was the fashion to tear out pages from the illustrated bible and paste them onto the walls – and often over the ceiling too. The murals so produced would naturally arrange themselves around some elevated theme: 'The Lives of the Saints' was the most popular. With such raw material, how could a dedicated artist fail?

The pages which followed each other when so dramatically stapled together were even more effective seen in panorama. There would be a proper mixture of busy detail: hordes of the common herd, idyllic rural backgrounds, mountains rearing up challenging and symbolic – all set around the radiant centrepieces, the saints themselves. A single figure, his body racked with pain, but with his eyes turned heavenwards and lit by a blend of trust and supplication – it was the face of a man who sees a glorious end to his struggles, the visage of a martyr about to enter upon his apotheosis.

Nothing shone like faded indigo or sepia in those gloomy caverns. There it would be, more radiant with every passing season: the ideal of self-sacrifice and its reward, the vision of heaven, witnessed and reflected from the walls. You would stand and gape until you were encouraged to move on by the officious custodian – the priest or his curate – who, like all clergy, were eager to see something in the plate. This pettiness notwithstanding, you came away shriven and strengthened in your faith.

The prime article of that faith was 'suffering'. It was an arduous road and it led uphill; that was why the mountains assumed such significance. You got the miles in, kept off fried food – nothing too scientific – and you raced whether officially or on the clubrun. But the one thing that sorted the men from the boys was the ability to hang on when you were dying, to find that little extra when everyone else was on their knees. You had to be tempered in the furnace of suffering; any deficiency could be made up and even transcended as long as you were prepared to stand the heat. As dogma it was perfect: simple to try but hard to prove. It depended ultimately not on the body or the mind, but on those upper reaches called the spirit. All the Greats had 'it', you only had to look at their agonised contortions. They had gone into that *Casse Déserte* of the soul and brought back a loftier durability, a higher dynamism. The forlorn truth was that most of us had ended up in cycling because we were no good at more conventional sports. We desperately needed to believe that success was possible without too much athletic ability.

Suffering was the invention mothered by this necessity, a half-truth blown up to encompass the whole. Your elders passed on the doctrine in the classic manner: example first then explanation. When you first presented yourself on a clubrun everyone would sooner or later try to burn you off; it was the baptism of fire, the first and essential lesson.

Only later did you explore its philosophical intricacy, its all-embracing promise. That fire was both inner and outer, you learned to savour it, to let it sear your body and your mind; for it was the flame of greatness that licked around you then, the very torch that you might one day carry to the heights of Revelation: Le col du Galibier, Izoard, Mont Ventoux.

Our faith was pure, our devotion impeccable, our vocations rock solid. Although Chris and I were hardly yet even novices, what could prevent us crossing the Channel to enter the priesthood?

6. The Working Men's Club

One of the great advantages of employment in the local library service is the midweek break. Every Wednesday offers the opportunity for a quiet afternoon's potter around Richmond Park. For those unfamiliar with West London, there is a large expanse of parkland just at the edge of the suburbs which is a godsend to cyclists and to many others. It has a five-mile perimeter plus inner connecting roads which are barred to motor traffic. The countryside – otherwise a 20-mile slog along death-trap arterials – is on your doorstep if you live that side of Big Ben.

On a grey, overcast afternoon before Christmas '98, I was returning from my weekly devotions when I came upon a slight acquaintance I knew from filmshows and jumbles. He was waiting at the lights on the exit road from Hammersmith bridge. As I came the other way I gave him an extra-cheery wave because I wanted to be recognised, neither of us having seen each other on a bike before. He responded in kind and our exchange lasted beyond the usual courtesy acknowledgement which kept me from taking in the real situation. As soon as I turned away I discovered that, far from being on his own as I had assumed, he was the front runner of a whole group. Strung out behind him two by two, all slowing for the lights, was a sight so unfamiliar, so unexpected, that I nearly fell off my bike in surprise – a clubrun.

Here, on a road temporarily closed to traffic, that old institution – moribund for so long that it was almost erased from memory – had magically resurrected itself in the form of a pensioner's outing. There was the familiar crocodile, the odd assortment of riders, but also the communal warmth, the shared ease of mutual enjoyment; it was somehow more than a collective, much greater than its parts. I sat up again and began waving each pair through with mounting enthusiasm – perhaps too much, because I was really trying to wave them down. I wanted to freeze the frame, to take home some keepsake of this remembrance sprung so unexpectedly back to life. The whole afternoon had suddenly been warmed and lightened by their presence.

I rode on still relishing the experience, but as my elation subsided I began to feel a rueful undertow. It occurred to me that all you met on the road nowadays was a single figure like yourself. A kind of exile had crept up on us as we came and went pedalling our own private furrows. We were solitaries now, hardly able to rouse ourselves from our introspections to greet each other, banished from that numerous, welcoming community that we had once enjoyed – or maybe never even known. The lack was tangible, almost grief – something important had undoubtedly been lost.

There is a marvellous sequence at the beginning of the film *Spinning Wheels*, a review of cycling in 1952, which shows a clubrun wending its way through sunbathed, car-free English countryside. Everything glows with well-being and joy. From today's perspective, it seems like a lost paradise, a Garden of Eden. The garden is still there but the peace is threatened at every moment by a hurtling tin can or the thunder of a juggernaut, and the way out to it is barred by the massed ranks of the same. The clubrun is no longer a viable means of reaching such sanctuaries and so has fallen by the wayside. As a teenager I enjoyed that golden era when we took the Garden of Eden for granted; the clubrun was the highlight of my week. In those days we were able to stake our claim to road space by dint of numbers. We were a presence to be reckoned with, deferred to by the very forces that now threaten our whole existence.

The traditional club which provided a welcome to all age groups and abilities, and was seen as such out on the road, has now become a rarity; it has given way to a mainly specialised racing fraternity with a sprinkling of our sisters. My friends in such clubs report that clubruns exist only in wintertime and are predominantly chain-gangs with no let-up. Only dedicated racing men are daring and robust enough to confront the menace of the open road.

The sad, unavoidable truth is that the roads are no longer open. An increasing volume and violence of motor traffic has not only forced the clubrun into the kerb, but also brought the club itself to the verge of terminal decline. The club and the Sunday run go two abreast, but the clubrun is the heart, the prime mover. I should think that most clubs have their roots in groups meeting to go for a ride, the bonds are always forged awheel.

The lack of freedom on the roads also has a damaging effect on the natural evolution of youngsters to club level. In the past there was always a halfway house between getting a bike and joining an official club – we used to form ad hoc clubs of our own. But now even this link is being eroded. In London you see gangs of youths rushing about mainly on the pavement; so they too are discouraged from actually going anywhere. This may have a lot to do with the nature of their bikes which are exclusively of the knobbly-tyre variety. These are, of course, the perfect vehicles for the normal rough-and-tumble of their play – but for little else. Such bikes are mere playthings, toys – which are easily laid aside once a moped or the chance to drive comes within reach. Increasingly, lightweight cycling ceases to be an option because it is less and less visible and more and more impracticable.

Down in the country there is at least the availability of roads which are relatively traffic free. While out for a ride one Sunday afternoon on my annual holiday in Somerset, I came across a group of teenage boys waiting for stragglers at the top of a hill. They were all red-faced and windblown and as I rode up from a side-road their attention was turned upon me. My first impulse was to stop and have a chat, just to dispense the words of friendliness and encouragement that I would have appreciated myself at the same age. But the city dweller's suspicion of teenage gangs made me settle for a wave and a smile. 'Ooh, a racer,' said one of their number, not entirely ironically. As it turned out, they soon caught up with me just as we began a long descent. They were all on old hand-me-downs, but invariably shod with MTB tyres. Even on the steep descent they were pedalling furiously; the run was obviously a harum-scarum rush from one place to another and the devil take the hindmost. Naturally I was using the slope for a spot of freewheeling and was almost keeping up with them. The last one through was the youngest, on the oldest, most dilapidated mount of the lot; his mudguard stays on the front were simply jammed inside the forks. Each one had a word or two as they came past, acknowledging our basic fellowship and I felt chastened for my standoffishness. I should have ridden on with them, shown them what a real bike could do, done a bit of PR, but the moment had passed.

The whole incident was evidence that the old, well-remembered enthusiasm was still bubbling up in odd corners, but it also prompted the realisation that only in the heart of the country were such jaunts still possible. Cycling as escape, as pleasure in simple mobility, is being nipped in the bud in all but the more sparsely populated areas.

The prospects are bleak on all fronts. The average newcomer rides the bike for him or herself and when they get tired of it they move on to something else; there tends to be nothing beyond this sole ownership and enjoyment. Clubs are no longer on show because the clubrun has been squeezed off the roads. The ladder to community is still in place, but the bottom rung has been splintered.

The situation looks bleak, but the bicycle is a low-tech survivor. The cycle industry is still intact, thanks to our good friends the mud-pluggers; off-road tracks are gradually creeping out across the country; environment and health lobbies are gaining in power. Our great love affair with the car is no longer quite so blissful, a certain estrangement is evident. The signs are that it might turn into the vicious split-up of our previous fling with the cigarette. One further bad health scare or an unnatural disaster might turn the tide irrevocably – look what happened to the roast beef of old England.

Of course, in the long run, the petrol-driven vehicle is a dinosaur as doomed as the fossil fuel on which it thrives. What will we do with its tracks and runways when the death throes set in? All those acres of tarmac, those great swathes cut through the countryside – will we zig-zag across the lanes to greet our peers across the central reservation? Or will we abandon them as forlorn monuments to an era of stupefyingly pointless travel? Whatever the case, there must be a golden era of Sunday runs somewhere over the flyover.

In my own latter years as a teenager, the clubrun was the focus of my whole existence. I wasn't part of the great teenage revolution which was gathering momentum in the '50s. Teddy Boys were generally older so I didn't dance in the aisles to 'Rock Around the Clock'. Skiffle also passed me by. I knew the 21s coffee bar in Soho, but only because it was opposite Moroni's Continental Newsagents where I bought my French magazines. Yet I was part of a smaller upsurge to popularise cycle sport, a movement which has borne a bitter fruit in the present day when the Tour of France has become a matter of common knowledge due to drug-taking. We seem to have lost our basic rights for the dubious honour of national headlines.

As I remember it, the Sunday run provided a special blend of the social and the competitive. Competitiveness is somehow implicit in one's relationship with the bike; it soaks up your best efforts and still asks for more. In its mute, passive fashion it is continually egging you on to surpass yourself. Add the outside ingredient of other riders and you have an explosive mixture. The competitive spirit is ready to burst forth amongst any gathering of cyclists.

Paradoxically though, it was the urge to compete which kept us all together. We loved the companionship but we also felt compelled to break away from it. You started off just trying to cling on but gradually you became fit and strong enough to force the pace in your turn. The group was constantly testing the mettle of its members and thus strengthening the bonds which drew them together. What was the point of getting to the café first unless the others were there to troop in behind you?

These café stops were the bedrock of the social side of cycling. As soon as twenty or so miles had passed beneath our wheels we would search out some regular stopping place, usually a lorry driver's pull-up. In those days the countryside was peppered with modest traveller's rests, far more than today, so there was ample choice. Our needs were as simple as the traditional fare: a mug of strong tea and a factory-baked cake or curly sandwich. The much maligned British 'caff' was certainly a rough-and-ready place, but our high spirits were such that it always seemed to offer a warm welcome with its steamy atmosphere. and tea urn gleaming like the tabernacle of a wayside chapel.

Lunchtimes, though, could often present another face. We would regularly descend upon rather more genteel eateries of the tea shoppe-cum-restaurant type where Home County worthies would be gathered, ties firmly knotted into starched collars, their wives demurely twin-setted. The leisure age was not even on the horizon and eating out, especially on a Sunday, was a formal occasion. With our trouser clips and scuffed shoes we struck a false note amongst all this gentility. Not of course that anything was ever said, but the waiter's frostiness would often speak volumes. The fact was that we were forced to go up-market by the single, iron rule of performance dietetics current at the time: keep off fried food.

On one showery spring afternoon, Bo turned the tables on such tyranny by calling for a pair of scissors immediately he sat down and proceeding to cut the legs off his sodden grey flannels to make an impromptu pair of shorts – afterwards letting the waiter dutifully carry off the remains.

From the start of the run there would be friendly chatter all the way down the line which continued for the first hour or so. But as soon as some well-known climb reared up or a sign for a traditionally contested town came near, the mood would change. Toe-straps would be discreetly tightened and the talk would die away; hostilities were about to commence. This was the serious business of the day which made the chit-chat and the camaraderie all the more light and effervescent.

Clubruns functioned as a kind of rolling academy for formal competition – a school in the sense of a 'school' of dolphins. Learning was by demonstration and imitation, with shared enjoyment. Along the way you would pick up how and when to attack and when to sit in; how to bluff and read the signs of others flagging, and above all the skill of riding hard in a bunch without bringing everyone down. At four o'clock in the afternoon, going into the burn-up for the finishing sprint, you would have spent a long, hard day in the saddle. A few Sundays of this and the continental classic, which begins with fresh faces and bright liveries and ends with a handful of tired and dirty men urging themselves out of the saddle to contest the final dash for the line, would not be wholly foreign territory to you.

Of course, road racing itself was born of clubruns, and even in these days of big-time sponsorship and worldwide media focus it still shows traces of those humble origins.

During the '70s I was a regular visitor to Belgium for the Tour of Flanders and in 1977 two of us went to Ghent as usual for that weekend. It was only at breakfast on the Sunday morning that we discovered the start was in St Niklaas, some distance away. We dashed up there as quickly as we could, but were only in time to catch the bunch setting off. The rain had been pouring down since the early hours and we came upon the riders dressed up to the nines in wet-weather gear, pedalling along in a great cloud. One might have expected glowering faces and teeth gritted against the spray coming up from the road, but, in striking contrast to the conditions, the whole cavalcade was buzzing with animated conversation. There was a festive gaiety in the air as though they had been released from the week's cares and were off to enjoy themselves together. It was, in fact, just like a giant version of what was happening all over the two-wheeled world.

The same clubbiness is present in one of the early sequences of *A Sunday in Hell*, when Merckx and his team ride down to the start into the rising sun. The day will undoubtedly bring its hard-fought battles and cut-throat tactics, but for the moment one senses that they are content to enjoy the fellowship and pleasure of just riding their bikes.

You sometimes see this same undercurrent reassert itself even during the heat of the action. When there is a sudden let-up in a chase, riders at the front of the bunch start looking around for other takers and, finding none, then form up into a solid phalanx across the road. The final day of the Tour is always run off in a similar spirit until things begin to hot up for the *Champs-Elysées*, but what club could sit still with the Eiffel Tower coming into view?

There is one sphere in which the clubrun still reigns supreme: early season preparation for these same hard men in their winter training camps. As soon as Christmas and the worst of the weather is over, the cycling press regales us with pictures of long chains of smartly dressed *coureurs* strung out two by two beneath a Mediterranean sun – a dream line-up in every detail, getting the miles in.

It could be said that the life of a pro is one long clubrun, punctuated here and there by the super luxury variety with crowds lining the route and prizes for the first few home. Then in the summer they all go on tours together. Theirs is the biggest and the most exclusive club in the world – that's why we all dream and scheme to stand for membership.

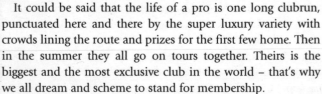

7. From Sepia to Vivid Colour

It still happens to me even today – a face is vaguely familiar, but I can't place it. A week may pass before the penny drops and the real association is revealed: what I had seen was a resemblance to Raymond Hoorelbecke or Claude Le Ber, some long-forgotten regional team-man splay-footed and hopeful on the starting line in a Tour preview decades ago. A face whose features had been burned into the retina of that omnivorous eye which x-rayed everything presented to it in *But-et-Club* and *Miroir-Sprint*, the French magazines.

There he is again, just managing a smile of satisfaction, but his brow wrinkling apprehensively: a figure from the '50s rescued from that ceaseless ebb and flow of memory which is only arrested by an instant of recollection. Once upon a time I could have dealt hordes of such faces from the top of my head; not only faces but legs, arms, shoulders – even elbows.

It was a challenge to be able to recognise every rider in a group, the front-runners back to the vague shadows of the hangers-on. The stars were too easy; the voracious mind sought more diverting play; it demanded to enter the frame, to dig into the reality behind the obvious.

Such intensity was more than an interest of course; it was an obsession, fruit of that adolescent surge which brings about the discovery of your own particular tastes and pleasures, that final stronghold of your own identity. And it was in tune with the spirit of the times – the youthful spirit at least. We war babies had known a very dim and enclosed world so that as we grew to maturity it was natural to search for light and space, broader horizons – and the bike was often the readiest of vehicles for that marvellous journey, a journey which inevitably led abroad.

To most people, the Continent was far away, out of reach financially and also rather forbidding. Things that have joined us to it since: the Common Market, Eurovision or even holidays abroad were then just a gleam in the eyes of the farsighted. You were lucky if you got a week in a holiday camp like Butlins, or a day trip to Southend. Hop-picking, not grape-picking was a big adventure in those days. Europe still held memories of war, and we had had quite enough of that. You couldn't read your magazines, though, without wanting to go – it was the heart's natural inclination.

France was the Shangri-La of cycle racing, but it was also just as hard to reach. Confronted with this problem we did the only thing possible: we decided to import. It was an effort doomed to a rather comical failure. For one thing, the Home Counties landscape remained obstinately itself. The bumpy hills, the winding lanes, the rounded hedgerows and trees would never transform themselves into those rolling plains, those dead-straight *Routes Nationales* with their spiky lines of poplars, much less the rearing monuments of rock where the final battles were fought. Our faith was impeccable, but it would not move mountains. Box Hill had one convincing hairpin, but that was all. Leith Hill seemed to go on and on for ever and Reigate felt like the Puy de Dome after you had been to Brighton, but nowhere could you tackle the semblance of a real *col*.

Names too were a frustration; the Anglo-Saxon and even Norman ones stood firm against the encroachments of Francophilia. All the Rons, the Harolds and Barrys would never have the euphony of Louison, Raphael or André. Stokenchurch, Monks and Nettlebed, though revered as sacred testing grounds, would never command the resonance of le col d'Izoard, Aspin or Peyresourde; just as High Wycombe and Lane End could never stand in place of Thonon-les-Bains or Briançon as hill stations. It was hard going in the Chilterns – and not only on the legs.

Even the small touches of French culture that did penetrate our lives seemed designed to mock us. My pal Blaise had an obviously Gallic name, but he just didn't have the appearance to go with it. He was chubby-faced, blonde – and Irish to boot. Every year there was the Victor Berlemont Memorial race and Gaston, his son, would come out from the French pub in Soho to do the honours. Here again the effect was smudged because our distinguished visitor looked every inch the bewhiskered English squire – nothing like the swarthy *patron* you might have expected. Life was green and pleasant however much you wanted it to turn azure and gold.

If Shangri-La proved difficult to import, this did not constitute a further reason to get up and go – oh no. As you were gradually initiated into the mysteries of the calling, it became apparent that you couldn't make the trip frivolously. The sacred soil was too important for that.

The only possible reason for going would be to embark upon a career; and for this there was a firmly established precedent. Like the mounting of a wartime raid or the initiation of a medieval knight, it involved a long and arduous preparation. You took the heaviest job in the Firestone tyre factory, opting for the night shift which was reputed to yield fabulous wages. You did as much overtime as you could get all through one winter and you saved every penny. By spring you would have amassed enough to take you across the Channel and keep you there for at least six months. Your first stop would be Paris in an effort to infiltrate the prestigious ACBB (Athletic Club Boulogne-Billancourt), a club well known for offering a place to foreigners – it had worked for that Irish interloper, Seamus Elliott, so why not for you? If this drew a blank then you would go to earth in the provinces and live off *kermesses* until one of the big team managers spotted you. That old boy with the peasant's beret and the look of a scheming cardinal, Antonin Magne – he would do.

This was the route of popular legend; but I was still at school, and though impressionable something in me baulked at the prospect of the tyre factory. So I sat it out at home with a growing pile of magazines and a much larger cloud of dreams. Bobet completed his hat-trick, then Walkowiak upset the apple cart with a win from the ranks of regional *domestiques* in 1956. The next year a youthful Jacques Anquetil swept to a victory which seemed to be a clarion call to all youth to stir itself.

I went over in the autumn of that year, 1957, having worked all summer to earn the money – nothing too ambitious, just a little sortie to Brittany to link up with Specs, who was already over there. I crossed on the night ferry to St Malo and spent a calm, moonlit night sleeping out on deck. Blankets were provided; it was all very romantic. Once disembarked I had only to ride a short way inland, to Dinan, and from there to a little hamlet where my host was already established. But such was my excitement and tongue-tied inhibition (and the inadequacies of a YHA map perhaps) that I managed to lose my way and did an increasingly hunger-knocked circuit of the place.

I kept riding on the wrong side of the road, especially when panicked by some oncoming 'put-put'. Where were all the racing men, I began to wonder. No gleaming *vélos* were to be seen anywhere, no dandified *coureurs*, nothing but those blasted *Vélo-Solex*, their riders waving fists and hurling abuse. I hadn't even found a proper bike shop – the one I did come across was full of the equivalent of our sit-up-and-begs. It was all a rather sorry anti-climax, gathering momentum with the waning of the day.

I was just about back where I'd started from and I still seemed as far away as ever from my destination. But what was that I could see approaching through the gathering dusk, the white bob of a massed-start cap – a fellow road-man at last? Would he acknowledge me, though, in the time-honoured British fashion? I raised my hand tentatively from the handlebars. He waved back, and then more enthusiastically. It was Specs out for a canter before dinner – I was home.

We repaired to the little inn at the crossroads, and that night

I sank into the feather mattress of a big, wide bed and felt a silence descend which absorbed everything. Even the hourly chime of the church clock became as insubstantial as an echo in my dreams.

I spent the next day happily in Specs's shadow; he had become a village celebrity. Unfortunately it was also the day of his departure. Left to my own devices I fell to scanning the local paper for an event. There it was, right on cue: *un grand critérium professionnel* at Lamballe, just down the road.

So it was that I presented myself one Sunday in early September to a man in the traditional beret sitting behind a card table set up on the pavement to take the money, halfway up the rise which led to the start/finish area and the stands where those fabulous creatures long known by their image alone were gathered, ready at last to be devoured in the flesh.

With my old hand-me-down iron (was it a Frejus, a Cinelli?) toshed up in a morose shade of grey from a tin of Robbialac lacquer; my equally forlorn *Grimpeur* shoes keeling over on their scuffed sides; with my trouser clips firmly in place and my home-made bonk-bag dangling on my back, I was a fairly representative late '50s clubman – victim and standard bearer of the collective inferiority-complex of British cycling. The B.L.R.C., known as 'the League', had dragged us out of the pre-war alpaca blackout, but its dire cloud lingered on; lots of people still rode bikes which looked as if they had been dunked in tar. A few visionaries had seen the light and word had filtered down; words are only words, however, what the spirit craves is illumination. Most of us had sustained ourselves over the years on the reflected glow of the magazines; but a man who has fed on shadows all his life can have little conception of real food. There I stood then, a poor relation come to the feast.

You could see the riders away up at the top of the hill; they were waiting their turn for a prologue time-trial. Just like the magazines which they graced, one's first impression was of colour – but this time also of vividness, depth and variety.

Schooled as I was in monochrome, I was unprepared for the vibrant reds and yellows and blues which assailed my eyes, nor was I in any way primed for the most spectacular colour of all – the brilliant gold of the legs and arms and faces. It was as if a golden florescence shone in and on them. They glowed with a special radiance even from afar. And there were so many of them, such an abundance; one on his own might have been digestible, but here were 30 of the same magical species.

They grew in stature and detail as I approached until they assumed the proportions of some mythical tableau. I was transfixed, I was overwhelmed. Although I kept on walking automatically, my whole body was frantically trying to come to terms with the marvel of this vision. Reality had suddenly outstripped any possible dream, the sustained and subtle shock was making my knees begin to buckle.

I could hardly credit the evidence before me even when these beings began to inhabit identities with which I was familiar: Hassenforder, Groussard, Job Morvan. What were all the other spectators doing? I wondered, were they feigning indifference, could they really be as unaffected as they seemed? The muted scales of blue and brown had fallen from my eyes and with them the long-cherished ideals of self-denial, devotion, suffering – the whole pious edifice melted away in an instant. I found myself in the blessed light of *reality*. Here was a more fundamental, a more vital order: a triumphant, brilliantly unrestrained paganism, a glorious celebration of life itself. I felt as though I had set foot on Mount Olympus; that I had come into the presence of the Gods.

Just then Raymond Poulidor stomped by to tackle the last gradient of the hill – another explosion of colour: the violet of his jersey against the dark, glowering head, the aureate musculature of the limbs – but above all, the pink of his Mercier. Pink – what a colour for a bike, it was really shocking. One was used to all manner of bright flams and lustres, but this had another quality, it was milky, yielding, essentially feminine. Why of course . . . it was the ideal colour for the machine – and the man, they made a perfect couple. Trust the French to apply a faultless logic, to have the flair to state the obvious. It's not by accident that they refer to the bike as *la petite reine*.

I rode back to the hotel in a state of high exhilaration, but there was a vague sense of apprehension also impending. My little monochrome world of reflected glory had been swept away irrevocably; I was now, for all my fervour, without a refuge, a hidey-hole. The true light had dazzled, but perhaps it had been too overwhelming, too drastic? Could I measure up? Had I got what it took to carry the flame? These large, searching questions were hanging in the air, though the warmth of the enthusiasm that suffused me held them at bay. The truth was about to test me. I was already on the verge of doubt.

8. A Legacy

All cyclists have a thing about their legs. We love our lallies; we even go as far as to fetishise them. Who was the first to take a razor to the hair of the lower limbs for appearance's sake? They may mean a lot on a personal level, but from a more detached point of view it has to be admitted that they are no great guide to ability. Some of the greatest riders in history have had little of note between hip and ankle.

Marcel Wust shows the kind of form that you might find holding up a billiard table, but what does that gain him besides a few bunch sprints here and there? While Luis Ocana, who gave Merckx a run for his money at the Master's peak and subsequently won the Tour in 1973 (sans Eddy) had the lower half of a scrawny teenage girl. There was a Dutchman in the '80s riding for Bianchi as a *domestique* who, I swear, had no musculature to his legs at all – just a bit of fat, skin and mostly bone. Coppi's great rides were done on pipe cleaners, so were Bartali's. Even to this day the strongest legs in the *peloton* tend to be the spindly ones; Richard Virenque's, for instance, are almost rickettsial. He brings a new twist to the paradox of the virtually legless champion: he spends most of his time out of the saddle. He seems to be able to honk his way up a whole *col*. Maybe the rest of his body has to make up for the deficit below waist level? Of course we all know now what powered his phenomenal climbing, but even that could hardly compensate fully for such unpromising limbs.

This is some consolation but it's of little comfort to those of us with dodgy pins. The great rides refuse to come and we're still left standing in the mirror's harsh glare. Mine are definitely of the pipe-cleaner variety and I'm afraid they've aged rather badly. Even as a teenager I bore an ill-omened blue protrusion below my left knee, and since then the rivulets and tributaries have multiplied on both sides, tracing patterns like those of a mature river delta – ox-bow lakes and all. I'm a pedalling geography lesson. It's very daunting to go out in shorts, but what else can you do in summer? One can only think of Sean Yates and wear one's veins with pride, discounting the fact that his citations were won on the battlefields of northern Europe.

I'm only talking calves here; I've never been less than happy with my thighs which have always bulked large enough to stretch a pair of jeans. It's the calves that let down the whole show. They just taper away ignominiously to my equally undistinguished feet – as documented earlier. Oh, for a well-turned calf.

My schoolmate Mick Riley had calves worthy of Michelangelo, and knew it too. He would pull up his grey flannels on the slightest pretext to expose these works of art, and flaunt their bulge and delineation. I had nothing to come back with but grudging envy and plots for revenge. Such unwelcome displays were almost as humiliating as feeling Yves Sougier's hard-on under the desk and being so outgunned as to refuse any reciprocation. Riley might have had the muscles but he was short on hard miles. He was, in fact, a lamb ripe for the slaughter. I plied him with the French magazines and lured him out to Brighton during the Easter holidays to tear those precious calves to shreds. On every climb it was elbow to elbow and the steadily escalating half-wheel until he shot backwards. Pure schoolboy sadism, of course; a favour which he returned with interest as soon as he was able.

Legs may be bones of contention, but they are also a universal language, a semaphore for those with the code. We strengthen our legs but also sensitise them. We become highly tuned to their messages and through them to yet more messages. Cyclists are all, to some extent, joined at the hip.

I remember catching up with Eurosport's transmission of the '98 Paris–Roubaix on a shot of some obscure byway of northern France – a few houses under a lowering sky and, streaming towards us, a line of riders; nobody special, the morning break. They took a corner to the right and the camera tracked along their legs as they came by. One could feel the crispness, the commitment of that pedalling. These men were going at it with the steady intensity of a paced but determined effort – the race was really on. Through an instant empathy with those legs one got the whole picture. I had joined the race at just the right moment, the forked antennae of my legs told me so, they were really crackling.

It was no accident that the cameraman had turned his lens in that direction; the prolonged leg sequence is part of the standard repertoire, not just for variety but to connect us with what we really want to see. Most of the production staff are enthusiasts anyway. They know what we root for because it is precisely what they relish themselves. A lot of the pleasure in these transmissions is in the direct, elemental connection with those legs going round. We pedal with them. No other medium can provide that experience and it is the reason why those blurred, often juddering images are so compulsive.

From time immemorial the lower limbs have always been looked down upon. The ancient Greeks taught that the head was the seat of all that was best in man, and that from there it was literally and metaphorically downhill all the way. The function of the legs was merely to carry the brain around, to say nothing of what lay between them. In the modern world we have reached such a level of pre-eminence over nature that even this modest burden has been largely eased. We can command vehicles to perform our movements and our limbs are more and more redundant. Yet of course, there is in us an even more ancient imperative for their use: the millennia of prehistory when they were our only source of movement, when we depended utterly upon them. Physically we are still Stone Age hunter-gatherers; 40 per cent of our anatomy resides in the lower limbs and 20 per cent in the arms. We are made to move under our own steam, to shift burdens other than ourselves. Hence as soon as we shook off the weight of hard manual labour and long working hours, the cult of jogging and general exercising took hold. We have to pay back our debt to evolution, our heritage demands its due. These appendages have their appetites too and there is a pleasure to be found in their indulgence, an enjoyment often termed 'heady'.

We re-discover the primitive in ourselves with the use of our legs, and this balances the over-sophisticated, perhaps decadent ways of advanced civilisation. When we set off on a clubrun or in a group, we are re-enacting the primeval ritual of the hunt. We are recapitulating the shared purpose, the co-operation, all the rigours and joys of an adventure – a necessary, indeed vital, adventure in those days. These rituals still persist in many forms, one thinks of fox-hunting or deer stalking, for instance.

The body repays attention; there is an exquisite pleasure in that sense of the fullness of the legs after exercise, that feeling of being firmly planted on the ground. Even the dull aches give a measure of satisfaction, for they are mementoes of a forceful ride. They may summon up old memories of cramping up in the cinema on a Sunday night and having to retire back behind the stalls to loosen up. Who knew of stretching exercises in those days? As a cyclist one never feels really happy on one's feet unless there is a degree of strength and resilience in the legs.

During my telly-watching days I remember once switching on the Tour and coming upon our old friend, Richard Virenque, leading a group on the lower slopes of a climb. They were charging through the ranks of goggling spectators and paying them no heed at all. It was still early days on the stage, but the racing was nonetheless fiercely engaged. What struck me was the contrast between the watchers and the watched. Some age-old knot of excitement is tied by such a cavalcade, it naturally draws a crowd and holds them. I am sure we have all felt that same hypnotic spell while standing by the roadside, even just witnessing some minor passage of arms.

65

Over for the Tour of Flanders one year, I stood at the top of a rise and from several rows back heard the scream of brakes and caught flashes of colour as riders prepared to meet a jagged-edged ramp further down the slope, where tarmac gave way to cobbles – a hazard formidable enough to unseat one of the motorcycle escorts earlier. But all the riders managed it faultlessly, their flimsy bikes and scantily-clad bodies vaulting and landing with animal grace and certainty. Those fleeting incarnations of speed and daring left everything in their wake seem lumbering and earthbound – certainly us flat-footed gawpers. As watchers we are made to feel our passivity, but we are also stirred by such intense activity. In the past, peasants just come up from the fields would have felt the same way about a detachment of Napoleonic cavalry galloping through on their way to battle; there is something very compelling about mounted men moving with urgent purpose.

Virenque and his cohorts were certainly mounted, but they provided their own driving force; they were 'in' and 'of' their mounts in a different way to horsemen. The strange thing was that this made them seem other than just rider and vehicle. At full pelt the bicycle empowers the legs and the whole body but also absorbs it; the two merge, becoming something larger than life – a composite akin to the ancient myth of the centaurs. It is said that the Greeks for all their philosophic acumen were so completely overwhelmed by the sight of nomadic tribesmen from central Asia riding horses (their own were too tiny to ride) that they took this enormous advance in locomotion, comparable to space flight in our age, to be a monstrous deformity and invented the myth of a creature half-man, half-horse. The Tour men fill us with the same awe and wonder, but we take the mythical creature for granted. What we see is men on bikes, but we respond perhaps subconsciously to a similar marvel, a mechanical centaur fully man and fully bike, a modern version of the old myth.

The man with enhanced shanks is a recurrent figure in folklore and mythology; all giants are – especially 'The Seven-leagued Boots' and so is Mercury, messenger of the Gods. The centaurs were also notoriously quarrelsome, taking it out on each other if there was no one else to pick on. Think of those massive bunch sprints where a lot more than just pushing and shoving goes on. Remember too how enraged you become when the traffic gets overbearing, or when some motorist cuts you up – to say nothing of those violent skirmishes which flare up when you are out in a group. The battle of the centaurs is never too far away.

Reduced to their common factors, myths have always been the collective desire/aversion personified. We have myths for all occasions and predicaments, large-scale general ones and small, private ones; they are all around and shot through the fabric of daily life. The all-pervasive media – a myth in themselves, perhaps – derive their power from purveying myths. Our mechanical centaur is a mythical figure for the modern age because he has the distinctly up-to-date gloss of being intrinsically 'two-faced'. He can distance himself from his lower half – he simply dismounts. Indeed everything conspires to encourage and exploit this duality because it is, of course, the basis of any civilised appreciation of the sport. All sportsmen are to some extent licensed beasts. In competition our modern 'centaur' is called upon to exploit fully his mechanically enhanced aggression – his beastliness – within the rules, but off the bike he resumes his normal humanity, he is expected to be modest and unassuming. Contrast the grim, hard-faced battler of the final miles with the nice chap on the podium. If he is allowed to have it both ways, so are we; his schizoid personality gives free rein to ours. As spectators our enjoyment is complete: we have our cake and eat it. There is no split in our minds because the two facets are joined in the man. We do not acknowledge the myth, it pierces straight with the speed of light to those inarticulate regions of our heart of hearts. That is why this mechanical centaur is such a powerful figure, his special status is taken completely for granted, it is swallowed whole. He is thus the perfect vehicle for our highest aspirations and our darkest impulses.

The truth is that as soon as we sit astride a bike or even think about it, our hearts open, we enter the realm of a myth which speaks directly to the essence of our being. Cycle sport is a whole mythology built upon that first simple discovery we all make when we wobble and weave ourselves into the realisation that on a bike our legs feel omnipotent and our feet winged.

9. Going Out the Back

In the autumn of 1958, when we were both going into our final year of the arts sixth, my colleague, Mick Riley, secured me an interview at his shop and I took on a particularly lucrative paper-round – 15 shillings (75p) a week. Mind you, it was hard graft: a council estate with ten blocks of four floors each, an hour's intensive labour from seven to eight every morning. On Sunday it was particularly gruelling because you had to go back for another bag halfway through. The net result, though, was that I was able to put down a deposit on a brand new frame plus a set of Mafac Racer brakes from Fred Dean.

Thus, at the age of eighteen, I emerged from my chrysalis as a fully-fledged clubman – and success came early.

We had turned for home on one of our routine Sunday circuits of the North Downs when we hit the formidable mass of Reigate Hill. There is a long, sapping drag, then a dip into the town and the real climb begins out the other side. We were tightly grouped as we engaged with the first slopes which are deceptively easy, but soon after the old level-crossing, where the gradient begins to stiffen, I just pedalled away. Never before had I shown such temerity, but my new bike – in full racing trim (mudguard-less despite vociferous protests) – had given me wings. I felt like Fausto Coppi: imperial, disdaining even that backward glance to confirm the damage. It was only as I embarked upon the last excruciating ramp that I dared to take stock of what was happening behind. There they all were, strung out back along the road, suffering the same throes that I was – but not one within striking distance. I only had to hang on over that final stretch and the *prime* was mine.

Coming over the top transformed me into a Tour hero at the summit of a *col*. I had made my first mark; perhaps I was on my way to becoming a legend too, if only in club terms. There was always talk of a certain Dave Treen who regularly scooped the pot when *primes* were gambled for in the old days. He would win almost as an afterthought, having passed most of the run up calculating his winnings. And as these things go, it was this foible which made him a legend rather than the outright ability to win at will. The only Treens I knew were Dan Dare's relentless foes in *The Eagle* comic strip. They were led by the Mekon, a green dwarf with a large head and cat's eyes who floated in mid-air on a pod. But however confused I might have been about the exact nature of my elevation, I was certainly floating myself that afternoon on my new yellow *vélo*.

This little bit of elation went to my head completely; from then on I was always trying it on and taking advantage. Matters came to a head on a subsequent afternoon when I launched the final sprint from way out on 52x14 whereas everyone else was on fixed wheels. Ron Chitty thrashed himself to a white-faced spectre to catch me freewheeling across the line and then denounced my impertinence loudly.

'Call yourself a sprinter . . . ?' he fumed disgustedly.

'He's only a youngster,' someone muttered in my defence, but the fact was that I had overstepped the mark. I could no longer depend on any indulgence now that I had to some extent gained my spurs.

Another element was contributing to my friskiness. We had gained a new member in the form of a lanky, fair-haired chap with glasses – a kind of blond Ray Booty – just back from National Service in Malaya. He was a protégé of Specs and hadn't touched a bike for the two years he was in the mob. Bo quickly fixed him up with his discarded special-built frame that had met its Waterloo in the Essex Grand Prix. This needed an extra-long seat pillar and an enormous extension to accommodate the newcomer who was called Alan Hawkins. He was no stylist and the awkwardness of the bike didn't help. With the advantage of hindsight, it now seems likely that my Reigate effort was a pre-emptive strike while he still had so few miles in his legs. Significantly he was still second over the top which underlined our implicit rivalry. Blaise couldn't have been present that day otherwise he would have pulled out all the stops to beat me however well I was going, simply because he had long ago established an ascendancy in that department and was always careful to maintain it. Keeping your place in the pecking order was a powerful motivating force, especially for young bloods who saw themselves as up-and-coming.

Mine was a full life with the paper-round, school work and cycling; classes were a kind of relaxation. Sometimes I would take a day off, just from the mad whirl of it all, get out of the Tube at Hammersmith instead of going in and have a celebratory cup of tea and a bun in the ABC cafeteria above the station. The rest of the morning would be whiled away in the public library and for lunch I would buy a Telfer's meat pie to eat cold during the afternoon show at the old Classic in King Street. I preferred French films; something torrid with Brigitte Bardot or perhaps Fernandel. French had been my number one choice for A level – due, of course, to my predilection for the country's sporting press. There were four subjects on offer, with English, History and Geography completing the list. Three was enough for university entrance, but I opted to do the lot because I knew I would only laze around in any free periods. It was a half-baked notion, but no one, certainly not the teachers, tried to dissuade me. The school had no great academic record and very little career guidance. I had simply persisted in education because I kept passing the exams. The world of work had little to recommend it in my small experience, although there were moans at home about bringing in a bit of money.

These occasional excursions to the cinema, together with the non-cycling part of the magazines and items picked up from the posh Sundays which I had discovered through work, had seduced me into a love affair with French culture in general. I was taken by the look of the French, their stylishness, the way the men dressed and Brigitte Bardot's penchant for getting undressed. There was also the sleepy village life with its inevitable cycle race, plus the lilt of the language itself; it was all an intoxicating cocktail.

With a good bike and my tail up, the next challenge was, of course, racing. Blaise had already ridden a few times the season before in an old shrunken Westwelve jersey. I remembered him pulling up hot and bothered on the third ascent of the hill around the Marlow circuit, and on being handed a bottle of diluted Ribena immediately choking and spraying the unfortunate donor. It looked tough and forbidding that racing business, but he didn't give up. Wheels were turning towards my own debut later in the year. It was decided that I should try my luck in tandem with Alan after we had had a full season to get fit. The die was cast.

My first race is lost in the haze of a sunny morning out in some unfamiliar neck of the Home Counties. What I can remember clearly, though, is the feeling of anxiety. The momentousness of the occasion gave everything a too-pronounced edge; so much weighed upon that matter-of-fact dressing up and turning out, as half-bored officials went through the motions of their routine chores. The ticking off of names, the orderly submission to the scrutineer, the pinning on of numbers, the strange half-nakedness of racing gear worn for the first time in public – all served to emphasise the raw nervousness underneath. It was as if we were being herded towards some obscure rite of passage which was none too pleasant, but was deemed necessary for our own good. We all seemed gripped by a dull, bewildered panic like cattle being loaded onto the slaughterhouse truck. Grave reservations hung heavily on the mid-morning air and eyes caught flicked instantly away. It was far from fun somehow, very much an ordeal.

I had been told not to push too high a gear on the hills and to ride around with the bunch. Everyone had played down the importance of this first try-out, but that did little to ease starting-line jitters. Once we were underway, however, a lot of the tension evaporated and pedalling calmed us. We proceeded at a brisk but orderly pace, there was no pushing and shoving, no obvious aggression, deferential good manners prevailed. There were a few half-hearted attacks, but in the main we all seemed intent on obeying the same advice: to stick together in the bunch.

Out in the midday sun it became hotter and hotter. There was something lulling about the wide, almost traffic-free dual carriageways that we followed. The heat piled down and then rose again from the tarmac in a gluey haze; time seemed to slow and slow. A feeling of monotony and pointlessness began to overtake me. We climbed a hill and I found myself getting out of the saddle rather than changing down. 'Use your gears, use your gears,' I heard a small voice admonish me in my head, but it didn't seem to matter much either way. Then suddenly I noticed the swirl of empty air behind me, I had slipped back through the bunch until I was on my own at the rear; the wall of backs and bikes and pumping legs was closing against me, I was going out the back. These hard facts, once realised, sealed my fate, the wall just pulled slowly and relentlessly away and there was nothing I could do about it. No resources came forward to reverse this crushing verdict. I was lost, cast adrift, forgotten. But by the same token I didn't really care, all I wanted to do was lie down and go to sleep on the cool grass verge. I felt completely drained. That was it then, no surprise first victory, no instant stardom, DNF. But such thoughts hardly impinged upon the need for respite from the infernal motion. I tried to take a drink from my bottle and found that my throat was so parched that I could hardly swallow. Once I succeeded in passing something down, it came to me that what I needed was food. Rooting in my jersey pockets I came up with a piece of fruit cake, but it tasted like lumps of brick. I had to keep drinking and drinking just to get a few bits down. After a while

I was able to lie back, dazed and disorientated, to take that ill-earned rest. Yet there was little comfort in it, the sun continued to beat down and there appeared to be no shade within any manageable distance. All I could do was shift about to take advantage of what little was offered by the sapling supporting my bike. It was a fitful doze, but after a while energy began to seep back into my limbs, and a little will. No search party would be sent out, I realised, no ministering sag wagon would arrive to pick me up; the only way I might regain the fold would be under my own depleted steam. Alan, of course, had finished with the bunch – comfortably.

It was a bitter and shaming blow. I had, of course, committed the beginner's mistake of forgetting to eat and drink, and fallen victim to hunger knock. The whole business was easily explicable but not so easily stomached. At least I had the whole off-season to come to terms with such an unpromising debut.

April of '59 found me lining up with Alan and Blaise for the Archer Spring Handicap which preceded the Grand Prix. We were riding for the Myriad RC because the Westwelve no longer had any official status. We were all in one of Sorian's hand-me-down shrunken jerseys and were shivering with the cold. Nobody had told us that we should at least be comfortable going into these early races, so we just turned out in the regulation short sleeves with perhaps a singlet underneath. Goosepimples rose like Himalayan peaks all over the bare flesh of arms and legs; no embrocation either, just the prospect of motion into a stiff breeze to thaw those blue, puckered limbs.

We started off at a fair lick. There were a few shouted appeals to get organised and a general business-like air at the front. The three of us did our bit coming through with the Actonia and the Archer riders who were prominent. We knew their stars like Baz Wells and the Archer trio of McQuater, Spellman and Smith, so we felt duty bound. The majority, however, hung back dumb and uncooperative. After about 15 miles of this we were out in the Chilterns and suddenly, round a corner, we came upon a sharp rise. I was caught in the wrong gear and immediately lost momentum, picking it up again only to hit a steeper section. I was going so slowly that I didn't dare change down and had to put a foot to the ground. After running a bit to a more level stretch, I was completely crushed by the realisation that there was a gallery further up and in the middle I caught sight of the familiar silhouette of a clubmate. Under normal circumstances I knew I would have romped up such a climb, but there I was shamefully pushing my bike. It was mortifying. All I could do was hang my head and get back in the saddle as soon as possible.

The moral shock completely winded me: another defeat was upon me. I was off the back again, but this time out of incompetence and half-heartedness. It was the same feeling though, the dejection of being dropped, and the same miserable doggedness took hold of me. It was a handicap, of course, so before long the middle markers descended in a swarm. They were all big, burly fellows going that much faster and with no time at all for some crestfallen little third-cat. I latched on to a few wheels but with no firm resolve so I was quickly dispensed with. I ploughed on my way for another mournful stretch until the backmarkers thundered through like a posse of tigers with the smell of blood in their nostrils. By this stage I was so demoralised that I couldn't have held a wheel even if I'd managed to get on one. I limped home along the rest of the course and on regaining the dressing rooms discovered that Baz Wells had managed to stay away and win the event – the first time a junior had ever done so. There we were then, at opposite ends of the spectrum: one coming home in glory and the other slinking in with his tail between his legs. My racing career was turning into a trail of mishaps.

As we were now serious racing men, we started going out on a Tuesday and Thursday when the evenings got lighter and this was far more satisfying than formal competition. We would take the Great West Road out to Staines and then on towards Egham. The outward leg we took at normal speed, two abreast, but as soon as we hit Tight Hill up to Egham Common it was flat-out and every man for himself. There was no doubt in such company and no holding back; you couldn't get dropped because you wouldn't let yourself, it was the old clubrun code of honour. Over the top it was bit and bit across the airport, and on every rise someone would peel off to attack. No quarter was asked or given; a controlled savagery became the order of the evening. We were like three men in a boat, each one trying to row the others overboard – but coming home to rejoice in having given and taken our best.

The next event we rode was run off around an undulating circuit in pouring rain, but it was reasonably warm rain, and though I remember my legs turning to mahogany at one stage, we all three of us were there to contest the bunch sprint. Blaise dug into his reserves to heave himself up to the front for a placing while I could do no more than stay with those around me. Alan was somewhere behind. It was a result which reflected the hierarchy established on the Great West Road. But all other considerations paled beside the fact that I had at last finished an event; I was no longer a hopeless tail-off.

Somewhere around this time we decided to ditch the Myriad RC and their shrunken jerseys and take up with the Chequers – a more prestigious outfit with the added advantage of a local clubroom. We duly presented ourselves and received a terse, offhand welcome from that great League pioneer and all round inspiration, Chas Messenger. The only other thing I remember about that venue was a visit from the Actonia in the form of Baz Wells and a heavyweight thug who came within an ace of landing me one for my impudent chatter. (Blaise defused the situation by exhorting him to do so.) Both our visitors wore motorcycle jackets which turned out to be an ominous portent. Baz was killed later that year while acting as a mobile marshal on the Tour of Britain.

Although I was doing A levels in June, I stepped up the training over the Easter hols. One morning I set out along the A40 for Oxford, but turned round before the town sign. I immediately found myself battling into a stiff headwind. On

Stokenchurch Hill I was passed by a sugar tanker making a laboured progress just a little bit faster than my own so I gratefully accelerated into its slipstream. Over the top the descent is gradual and I found that I could easily stay with it. After a while, I poked my nose out into the wind again and found that I had worked up such a sweat as to be in danger of a chill if I dropped back. There was every incentive to stay put because the vehicle belonged to a firm in Hammersmith; potentially I had a tow all the way home. Neither was the driver making any move to get rid of me. It was a perfect motor-paced workout, and I was back indoors shortly after lunch – nearly a four-hour hundred.

In-between times we thought we'd give the West London chain-gang a spin instead of our usual Tuesday night sortie. They met at Kew bridge and sallied forth through Kingston to Box Hill. There was a big group, probably over thirty riders, including most of the active members of the Chequers. Keith Mernickle, the cyclo-cross star, was rumoured to occasionally put in an appearance.

All was going well until we came under the red kite for the Leatherhead sign. It was a downhill approach so the speed was high, and we were fanned out across to the white line. I was sitting comfortably in the middle, but judged that I ought to be nearer the front runners if I were to steal it. As I moved up, one of my new colleagues from the Chequers came out of his saddle to do the same and I had to brush past him. The result was a mass pile up; he lost control and brought down everyone behind like a house of cards. Another Chequers rider flew across the face of the oncoming traffic into the opposite ditch – only a miracle saved him from serious injury. When I got back to this scene of carnage, I was blamed loudly and vociferously by my wronged clubmate as the sole cause of the debacle when he was as much to blame. I was proved guilty on the spot for want of a ready answer. Only the calming influence of another, Bob Garner, saved me from an imminent lynching. Nobody, however, was seriously hurt and no bike irreparably damaged. They were all able to continue, but I felt as if I'd been sent to Coventry. After that we judged it best not to show our faces again at Kew Bridge.

We did, however, persuade the Chequers to try our route a few weeks subsequently, and we set out mob-handed for a change. It was shoot-out time on Tight Hill that evening and we had the drop on them. From the bottom we went as hard and as fast as we usually did so that over the top we were on our own. Mick Burnett, Johnny Stallwood and Derek Moss got back on as we crossed the common, but a few attacks on the following slight rises put paid to them. We came home relaying each other in quiet triumph. We never saw the Chequers out again either.

On another night across the airport, a strange thing happened: Blaise and I lost Alan. We assumed that he had fallen behind with mechanical trouble and would soon catch us up. But after a while, when he didn't materialise, it began to dawn on us that he'd perhaps slipped away and was ahead. This hardened into certainty as we began working at full bore to bring him back. But he still refused to appear on the horizon. Blaise was on an 'off' night and couldn't come through with his usual vigour. Nevertheless we both felt that we should have been able to catch him – it was two against one, after all. Our chase became more and more desperate and headlong; certainly on my part because I was relishing the opportunity of making Blaise suffer for a change. A sense of disbelief continued to hang over our efforts, though; could it be possible that he was showing us a clean pair of heels? As we turned into the Great West Road, this seemed to be increasingly the case. After the sprint which I won comfortably (Blaise showing commendable grace in putting up a show) we decided that the only way to resolve the enigma would be to go straight round to Alan's house. Sure enough, he was there, and had been for some time. We made light of the matter, pretending that our only concern was for his safety, but both of us went home with slightly heavier hearts. Neither of us – though we didn't admit as much to each other – would have had the nerve to try such a feat, much less pull it off. The balance of power had shifted quite perceptibly; indeed, there was something prophetic about this turn of events which we were to discover later in the year.

On a clubrun one bright sunny morning out in the Chilterns we came across Mick Riley after he had just finished sixth in a thirds and junior event. He had come out with us a few times only to be soundly thrashed for his pains, but had shown some promise. Now he was suddenly cock of the walk having been lured away to the Vélo Club Sacchi and their fancy imitation *Bianchi* jerseys à la Coppi. What was really hard to stomach was the fact that he had managed to stay with the Archer triumvirate of McQuater and co. over Kop Hill, which was absolute murder – all on his rickety old bike. Kop has a lot in common with its namesake, the notorious *Koppenberg* in the Tour of Flanders. The mere mention of it turns your legs to jelly. Riley, the sprog whom I'd nurtured – admittedly for my own ends, but nurtured nonetheless – had turned into a precocious monster who was now talking down to me from several rungs higher up the ladder. I made my escape as soon as possible, since I knew that I would get more than an earful next day at school. But the galling suspicion was born that it was perhaps he who was endowed with that natural class which I was still vainly searching for in myself.

We next rode a thirds event around the motor-racing circuit at Crystal Palace on a rainy Sunday afternoon. There had been a huge pile-up in the final sprint of the junior race. A good proportion of the field had come down and an ambulance arrived just as we were called to the starting line. Undaunted, the madcaps took off at a sprint and on the first few bends riders were skittling away on all sides. Things settled a bit after that, but years of scorched rubber being laid down at the corners plus a steady drizzle had turned them into an ice rink. Our wheels became skate blades ready to slew sideways at the slightest inclination. You quickly learned not to sit too tightly on anyone's wheel because it only took the blink of an eye to find them spreadeagled across your path. Nonetheless, lots of characters were haring about as if that tarmac were a velvet cushion. It was a nervous race, torn between hanging on and staying upright, but I remained fresh enough to work my way to the front for the final gallop. I thought I'd got fourth or fifth when my clubmate, Bob Garner, came up behind and persuaded me to ride round again since he was a lap down. When I arrived back and checked the finishing list my number wasn't even up. What could I do though – it looked as if I'd only just come in. Another lesson learned the hard way.

Then there came a major confrontation with the Archers around the Marlow circuit. It was important enough for us all to go down by train to save our legs. Four times up the back of Marlow Hill was a stern test by any measure – Blaise knew it from the previous year, and he went well, contesting the first prime with Tom McQuater, the Archer's leading light. The second time up was a bit stiffer and on the third I was shot off with a few others. We crawled around the final lap and I veered wildly off my line in the final sprint trying to stop some sturdy junior coming through. Blaise and Alan were in the winning break which McQuater emerged from to take first place. But for my *défaillance* we would have matched them at least on personnel.

From that point on there seemed to be only eighty-milers on offer and though I always finished it was with the tail-enders. The extra distance was always too much for me. Towards August the season was running out of steam. School had finished and I took a factory job in Joe Lyons, the source of the famous fruit pies which were a staple of our café stops. But producing them was entirely different from eating them. It was awful: the noise, the stench, the gloom, the relentless monotony of taking trays off a conveyor belt, the clock hands which seemed stuck to the dial, the reject pastries that you ate out of boredom until you were sick, the horrified disbelief that life could come to such a leaden standstill, the remorseless weight of the day that pressed down on you in the early hours and only lifted as going home time approached – it was purgatory. I had done odd days in Telfers making sausages, but the grinding oppression of a full week plus Saturday mornings sapped something more than the body.

I still went training but the urge to race fell away as did the choice of events. We began putting our names down for anything on offer just to have somewhere to go; clubruns too had fallen into decline. All the top men, Bo, Ron Chitty and Blissett had suddenly gone into retirement for various reasons.

So it was that we congregated for a top-class event, a hundred miles around the Chilterns which included several internationals on the start sheet, notably Jim Hinds. As it happened, the changing-rooms were in the old Wycombe community centre where Chris and I had first discovered the racing scene – an irony which only became apparent from the vantage of hindsight.

It was a suicide mission and we knew it, but that took the pressure off. We could just go through the motions and enjoy ourselves – or so we assumed. Indeed, after a few miles out along the A40 we took off up the road, knowing that it would be our only chance of showing a clean pair of wheels to such exalted company. We were obvious jokers, and the joke wore thin after a while. We had to let ourselves be hauled in, and nobody was laughing.

When we turned off into the lanes a more purposeful mood took hold. The bunch drew in upon itself and the speed began to rack up mile by mile. Every man and machine began to play a finer tune as we sped along those snaky, undulating byways. The intensity of effort became an abstract music; it was an orchestral sound: the whirr and tinkle of transmissions, the swish of limbs, the creak of metal under duress, all set against the high pitched drone of so much rubber scraping on tarmac. I had heard that air before but never so fully, never so compellingly because, of course, I found myself dangling at the rear, contemplating the familiar wall of broad backs, and remorselessly pumping legs. But just at the moment when I had fallen completely under the music's spell my body gave notice that I was about to lose my place. Once more and for the last time (though I didn't know it then) I was going out the back.

10. A Living Mythology

The mythical realm is always with us. Myths are adult fairy-tales; they express our deepest fears and joys, our finest aspirations and our utter aversions. Who has not traded in 'urban myths' at some time or other? We have long-since laid aside the classical model except as a handy glossary for names and characters; Oedipus survives as the Oedipus complex, for instance. Of course, the whole vast edifice of psychoanalysis is a mythology, as is Marxism – all the more evidently now for being on the wane. Few myth systems are durable enough to withstand time – 'love' perhaps, or 'war'? They need not be confined simply to stories either, myths at their most seductive incorporate music, objects, images, practices; the really big mythologies like religion are a mixture of everything possible. In the new global village of communication overkill, we live in a tropical rain-forest of proliferating mythologies. Anything that draws attention to itself by becoming a cluster of ideas, feelings, associations, is on the way to small-time mythology.   But we cannot catch a glimpse of the large, all-embracing myths of the age – the treetops which filter the light – because we are lost on the forest floor. If we look around us, however, we can spot the ground-level stuff like rock 'n' roll and football. Sub-cultures stand out more obviously since they are confined and specific. In these spheres we can recognise our myths even as we live them out – cycling is such a case.

According to Rudolf Otto in *The Idea of the Holy* every living mythology is based upon some kind of inner truth finally beyond the reach of words, something which has to be experienced. This is true of cycling inasmuch as the simple act of pedalling gives access to a fuller sense of life. Scientific studies show that rhythmic exercise like cycling increases alpha-wave activity in the brain, producing a calming effect similar to meditation. In the saddle, all keen cyclists become more or less unwitting mystics. The love we feel for riding our bikes is a foretaste of that pure life-abundance which is at the end of the mystical quest. Our levitations may only be low level – less than the radius of our wheels – but they are, nonetheless, a significant step up, and are readily available. That thoroughbred, that trusty old iron, is basically a devotional aid, a prayer wheel.

This everyday mysticism is, of course, completely democratic; we need not be Tour de France stars to enjoy its fruits. In fact, top-rank professionals present the outward, official face of the inner illumination. They are the apostles of our road-spun creed. It is their vocation to embody and demonstrate the higher levels of enlightenment and their ministry consists of ritual celebrations dispensed throughout a traditional calendar of feast days and festivals. Sometimes they may appear to be just going through the motions, but usually our evangelists rise to the big occasion.

Races are the incremental units of our mythology. They represent a special time set aside for testing and proving what man is capable of; they are a rite of renewal and affirmation. The great races demand the best and in so doing usually bring it forth. On the starting line the clock is set back to zero and the whole field is granted a new life, a fresh chance to find that within themselves which is timeless. Great rides stand forever, yet in their peerlessness they are all the same. A single race may launch or crown a career, or even redeem it. There is everything to play for and everything to lose because that chance may never come again. One man may achieve the defining moment of his life and the others will merely live to ride another day. For its duration the race mirrors the lifespan we all share; it is the individual and common life played out on a small, intensified scale. What it demonstrates is something that we all recognise: the opportunity which life offers us at every turn to rise above ourselves, to become what we really are. That edifying spectacle has an inner meaning and significance: the power of a secular sacrament to reveal what is concealed in the ordinary run of things – the real, the holy.

When we see a relative unknown like Oscar Camenzind hold off the established hierarchy to become world champion our hearts are stirred. But this is as nothing compared to the next weekend, when, given wings by his new rainbow jersey, he soars away from the same field on the wooded slopes of Lombardy. We feel that tremor of excitement which might herald the emergence of a new *campionissimo* – just as Hinault's double in the '77 Ghent–Wevelgem and Liège–Bastogne–Liège announced a master coming into his own. Like the children of Israel in the Old Testament, we live in fervent hope of the redeemer's coming, some new Coppi or a Merckx who will change the world for ever.

There was an even more telling footnote to this triumphant end to the '98 season. *L'Equipe* described how an elegantly dressed old man was waiting with tears in his eyes for the arrival of the new champion at Zurich airport. He turned out to be not an aged relative or even a close friend, but the last Swiss world champion, Ferdi Kubler, winner in 1952, 46 years previously. He wanted to be among the first to greet his young successor. Now here was a moment which bore witness to the power and depth of the mythology underpinning cycle sport. The old champion, who is approaching his eighties, explained that he had spent the whole afternoon watching the race and was overwhelmed by the final verdict. It was a dream come true for him to see the jersey pass to a compatriot after such a long wait. Could there be any finer or clearer measure of the love and devotion he felt towards the sport? That generosity of spirit could only have been founded on deep resources of pride and satisfaction with his own career. If he was able to summon up such emotion so many years later, to make such an eloquent gesture, what must his racing days have been like? These glimpses of what such events mean to the participants endorse the feelings that they arouse in us, mere spectators; they confirm, too, the sense of a living communion which is open to everyone.

All the great races at their most enthralling become narratives of spiritual discovery. The winner not only conquers his rivals, he finds some unprecedented resources within – he conquers himself. Pantani's Giro/Tour double of '98 outshone the dire circumstances of its completion by the marvel of his physical rehabilitation, but mostly through the fighting spirit which made it possible. Stephen Roche's sublime courage in coming back to Delgado on the climb to La Plagne in the '87 Tour showed the same sort of inspiration which would later in the year place him briefly on a par with Merckx. Examples crowd in from every era. In more recent years, when Andrei Tchmil broke away in the '94 Paris–Roubaix, what started as another seemingly fruitless sortie steadily grew into a triumphal progress to victory, the fanfare of a new champion asserting his true worth by riding his former boss, Museeuw, into the mud. This was the crucial breakthrough for a man who was thereby flying free of various subtle forms of oppression: his refugee status, the stigma of a cut-price entry into the pro ranks and his years of submission to Museeuw. It all fell away as he surged on across the cobbles; that victory had a moral weight which matched its physical brilliance. And hasn't he lived up to it since?

Of course all sport has the capacity to uplift and instruct. In fact the last half century has seen the sporting arena gradually usurp some of the prerogatives of the Church. What else can we conclude about the increasing sportiness of modern dress – the trainers first of all, then the tracksuit trousers (shorts in summer) plus the ever present tee-shirt and baseball cap? Even if we never visit a gym or a track, most of us genuflect before the shrines of the athletic. God's lingering demise has made us all into spartan existentialists; we are more focused on the here-

and-now than on any prospect of an afterlife. A trim body has become more than a fashionable ideal; exercise and a healthy lifestyle are now a necessary hedge against the dying of the light even as they reveal a covert recognition of mortality. Sport and sportiness have become a popular folk religion.

Decades of wholehearted consumerism have swept away the old pieties of the parish church and Sunday worship. We turn more readily now to the telly, that handy sideboard cathedral, which ushers us into huge extravaganzas of body-worship like the World Cup or the Olympics. Our souls are regularly captured by these orgies, they give us a more expansive sense of participation. We feel a patriotic identification with something larger; we are lifted out of ourselves by that electronic benediction.

On the Continent, however, the passing of power has been more gradual since the Catholic Church has deeper roots – even in matters of *le vélo*. It might be said, for instance, that the Tour de France took hold as smoothly as it did because the populace already had a taste for sumptuous processions of a devotional kind. Watch any start or finish today and the vestiges of Catholicism still catch the eye: that odd rider here and there making the sign of the cross. Okay, so they are mainly Italian or Spanish – but Ullrich and Zabel too? Ex-communists from behind the Wall?

There is an undoubted affinity also between the disciplines of race-preparation and the spiritual exercises laid down by closed religious orders. As recently as the end of the '70s, Kelly and Roche were immediately more welcome and adaptable in France than their UK counterparts because they had been brought up in the faith. They were good Catholic boys, just like Eddy Merckx. Those Irishmen knew all about the mortification of the flesh and the redemptive powers of suffering – hadn't they been weaned beneath replicas of the crucifixion? It was easy for them to accept the monastic regimes imposed upon young novices; they knew in their bones that sainthood was a necessary prelude to stardom, that the Almighty looked after his own.

On a broader front, cycle sport has held up its own small mirror to this relentless erosion of religious influence. After the war it bore the trappings of the old, largely Catholic, mythology and has since been embraced by the technologies which are giving birth to the new. By the '50s racing gear had been standardised on a vaguely clerical model: a soberly coloured jersey – like the priest's chasuble at Mass – over a black undergarment deferring to his ankle-length cassock but necessarily reduced for sporting purposes to long, black woollen shorts. On the feet another nod towards the church: black pumps. Trade names were artfully woven into the colours of the jersey, almost apologetic in their discretion. Come the Tour, a simple label was all that was permitted on a national or regional jersey. The whole outfit was topped off by a small, peaked biretta in foldaway cotton. During the intervening years these vestments have been gradually coloured in and jazzed up until we arrive at the contemporary version: a chaotically multicoloured, logo-splattered disguise, as gaudily anonymous and threatening as that of a tribal dancer or a voodoo shaman, hidden behind shades and a glossy shelled helmet. Most identifying traits have been sacrificed for the composition of an eye-slashing corporate cypher that's only partially human, a demon puppet from the techno-marketeers who are computer-generating totems for the new millennium.

Emerging mythologies traditionally annexe what is left behind by those in decline; Christianity itself was built upon the foundations of the old pagan festivals. Perhaps, by an ironic turn of the wheel, we are witnessing the revival of those same primitive values: the slave culture of ancient Rome where the plebs were diverted by watching men fight to the death. Is the spirit of paganism reasserting itself in Simulation print? Have our high priests become mere faceless gladiators, putting their lives on the line for transitory fame and wealth?

Rudolf Otto's second condition for a living mythology concerns its ability to explain the universe, to give a picture of creation. Cyclists, in line with most other groups and individuals, turn away from the ever-mounting complexity of life in general and the deepening sense of awe at the mystery of the cosmos – even of life itself – to do their own thing. It might seem like a 'head in the sand' response, but I would interpret it more as a 'head held high enjoyment' of what is known and trusted. The cycling world is therefore a world within a world, a little planet of its own which even reflects geophysical reality. At its white-hot core, taking up an unstable residence, is the current leader of the FICP (*Fédération Internationale des Coureurs Professionels*) rankings. Only the most robust and hardy can survive there, the pressure is immense and the merest seismic tremor will dethrone him even in the off-season. The dense, fluid nucleus is made up of the professional *peloton*, and around them the sponsors, the managers, the *directeurs-sportifs*, *soigneurs*, mechanics – all the personnel who take to the road with this deluxe chain gang. Then there are the officials of the governing bodies, the race organisers and national associations, filtering outwards to the media and a host of manufacturers and retailers – and from there on out to the great collective, the less-dense outer layer which is made up of devotees and enthusiasts who practice or follow the sport for their own pleasure.

This world has a luminous aura like the earth's atmosphere which is made up of all the folklore, the legends and all the conscious and unconscious memories and aspirations of the great tradition down through the ages. Cycling is forever looking backwards; it has an obsessed fascination with its own history which matches boxing and cricket. A recurrent feature of the magazines and books is a comparative study of the heroes of yesteryear with those of today and the compilation of a final and definitive hierarchy. The French publish a steady stream of archival material, learned conjecture and vivid description. In Italy you can still buy videos of the Coppi–Bartali era from news vendors in the street and the largest selection of glossy monthlies of any country.

We are, of course, not exactly short of such literature in the English-speaking world. Through magazines and books we are constantly invited to dwell upon the acts of the apostles of our sport. In fact – and this is the underlying thrust of such reading matter – we can freely imitate them by answering the adverts for their bikes, their team kit, every last little fetishistic bit and bob down to the suits they wear for team presentations. The spin-off industry, like some fawning shop assistant, draws us further and further into our wildest wish-fulfilment fantasies. We can take to the road now as fully authentic in livery and mount as the most exalted champion. Poseurs were once scorned with all the vehemence of suppressed envy – but not any more. The official line now is active encouragement. 'Everyone's doing it' is the implicit message. Our slavishness has come out into the open. Personally, I can't help admiring those more austere (and richer) types who obviously insist upon plain, logo-free garb.

I call it 'reading matter', but the essence of these publications is pictorial; the action shots which adorn covers and all the inside pages are what sell magazines. Coffee-table books, too, are on the increase. Stills continue to have an edge over the moving image simply because of their convenience and availability. By way of sharpness of register and composition, a good picture – and this is a highly developed art form – beguiles the senses in a uniquely powerful way. The instant, the look, the overall feeling, is immediately sucked in by the eye thus giving a depth of insight and understanding that no other medium can match. We can be easily drawn in because we are at our most suggestive threshold; the simple act of scanning a photograph is undoubtedly introspective and self indulgent, much to the delight of the hidden persuaders. Pictures are 'free' tickets to that hall of mirrors known as fashion which entrances the young and exasperates the old. But all the apeing and posing that they stir up in cycling also has a positive benefit: it can open up a more impersonal access, beyond identification and mimicry, to the mystery and exaltation of competition at those rarefied upper levels. We may get a sense of the marvellous which deepens our appreciation of the calling and returns us enriched to the now inviting prospect of riding our own bikes.

Once there, we enter the realms of that time-honoured but unacknowledged repertoire of mime and dance – the classical ballet of graceful pedalling. Have you ever noticed how self-conscious and formal the simple act of getting out of the saddle is? We are constantly playing up both to ourselves and to that unseen multitude who are holding their breath by the roadside. There is a concise style book of acceptable comportment awheel, which is being constantly and subtly updated. If you should ever catch a glimpse of some race footage from the '60s, you will notice how the *peloton* looks like a convention of nodding dogs. Our own Tom Simpson, for example, was a world class nodder. These days only those on their way off the back give even a hint of a nod. It's completely passé, like wrapping your spare tub in an oilskin cape; strictly for ageing dodderers. Gilbert Duclos-Lassalle was the last of the old time nodders in the pro ranks. He had perfected the rolling nod which was an added mark of distinction and his absence has left a wavering hole in our screens.

All our personal idiosyncrasies form part of the atmosphere, the *ambiance*, which is the subtle maintenance of our little world. The air we breathe is pure mythology; it may not be quite as intoxicating as it was in our youth, but it is always bracing. Up in the stratosphere dreams are born which gain shape as intention and then drop to earth as action, burrowing through the layers with the dreamer on a leash until he finally shoulders his way into the inner sanctum. There is a constant circulation from the ethereal to the material and back again. Eventually we are all exhaled to rejoin the dreams that sustain us, none but a tiny few leaving a trace upon the air.

Otto's third condition for mythology is the social prospect – the ability to bring about the validation and maintenance of an established order.

Here our mythology comes a cropper. After decades of stability and apparent probity our establishment has been exposed as corrupt and our standard bearers revealed as cheats, driven not just by human will and application but by chemical means, their transcendence achieved through hormonal interference. It is clear that the whole upper echelon are guilty, with the connivance of everyone around them up through the ranks of the international bodies and the big promoters to the figureheads at the top. The established order has been shaken as never before and is still shaking. A wholesale and long-term duplicity has been laid bare. Our living mythology has been exposed as a two-faced deity: on the one hand a gracious muse of inspiration, but on the other a hideous monster who devours its children.

We can no longer deny the evidence. Its repercussions and confirmations reach us daily through the good offices of the news services. We can no longer hide behind the denials and evasions of our higher officials; indeed, such footwork stands revealed as the root of the canker. The taint keeps spreading outwards until we must face the fact that we are all guilty, even if it is just by passive complicity.

As early as the Flèche Wallone in '94, when the Gewiss trio of Furlan, Berzin and Argentin simply rode away from everyone else, it was blatantly obvious that something was amiss. Furlan had already won Milan–San Remo in fine style, and Berzin went on to pocket Liège–Bastogne–Liège following up with the Giro later on in the year. Since that *annus mirabilis* his performances have sombred beneath gathering clouds of unanswered questions. Furlan never showed the same form again and retired after another few seasons. Argentin had already handed in his notice and popped up later in team management. There seems little doubt now as to the old campaigner's lore that he was passing on. At the time the Gewiss team's ascendancy was put down to the superiority of Italian training methods, but we can now see that this must have been laptop lies. The journalists must surely have known;

they were, of course, part of the cover-up, tied by the code of *omerta* which kept most of the brotherhood tightly buttoned up. Ever since Moser's hour record in '84, under the supervision of Dr Conconi, medical practitioners had moved more and more to the forefront of team support staff becoming the same sinister figures whose leading lights are now helping the police with their enquiries. The much applauded renaissance of Italian cycling seems likely to fizzle out in the glare of courtroom showdowns.

The Millennium season started under the flag of truce waved by Armstrong's squeaky-clean Tour victory and he managed to reprise the feat. But it is an uneasy peace, siege guns are rumbling in the background all the time. Efforts are being made to carry on as normal, yet new revelations and indictments are continually breaking out like sporadic small arms fire. The sport is in crisis; it has become like one of those international trouble spots which grate away at our nerves, reminding us all the time of our powerlessness.

As rank and file fans we have also come under suspicion; some of the mud has inevitably stuck to us and we are assumed to be guilty by association, as indeed we know ourselves to be. Our sport and especially the Tour de France – or most people's image of it – has become a watchword for abuse when it previously enjoyed high esteem. Not that our reputation has ever been spotless; those with a longer memory will recall a similar crisis when Tom Simpson died in 1967, two years after becoming BBC Sportsman of the Year. Anybody with experience knows that drug taking has always been an undercurrent in the sport. We even acknowledge it amongst ourselves with knowing references and cynical asides. But our complicity goes much deeper than mere knowingness. Behind it lurks the suspicion that we would probably do the same in their shoes. What are those riders but the most vulnerable playthings of that drive to transcendence which we all feel? The ruling passion of our sport has drawn them up into those misty peaks where the sublime can easily shade into the malign. Our human motivations, for all their masks, are as coldly unscrupulous underneath as Mother Nature herself. The individual, if he is not careful, will always find himself being offered up by the herd. Darlings of the crowd have an awful habit of turning into its sacrificial victims.

We are now paying the price for all that easy facetiousness, and it hurts. If we can feel it at grass-roots level, what must the riders and officials be going through? From top to bottom we are all paralysed by the appalling extent of the problem and the threat it poses to our little world. Who is going to clean out the Augean stables? Nobody from within them, that seems certain. Officialdom seems busy keeping up appearances, desperately intent on damage limitation, but succeeds in nothing more than a demonstration of their utter impotence.

Our only hope seems to reside with the police who in their dogged, blinkered fashion might provide the Herculean input by ferreting out some clue which will incriminate one of the big-wigs – and then by setting them at each other's throats reduce the whole shaky edifice to ruins. Then, perhaps, we will realise just what has been lost, what has been frittered away by a thousand duplicities, and begin rebuilding. Look what happened to the BCF. A real catastrophe will be our saviour because it will galvanise all the popular support and goodwill which is there in the foundations of the sport. Cycling is much more than the aberrant behaviour of its most visible practitioners. While these matters either blow up or blow over we can only keep riding our bikes in solidarity with the vast majority, who, being the real establishment, persist in that practice which is the crux of all order – by simply turning a clean pair of pedals.

And so we are brought inevitably to the fourth function of an adequate mythology: the centering and harmonisation of the individual – which is precisely achieved, of course, by riding our lightweight cycles.

The bike is a centering device par excellence. We are framed between two wheels, perched above the hub and on the rim of the turning world. We are moving yet at rest. We have slipped gravity's heaviest chains and twirl happily on its swing. We feel our individuality to its full and thus the world opens to us. We may find that original childlike sense of freedom and wonder, discovering ourselves again; ourselves as we have always been. All this goes on in us if we watch, but we really don't need to bother since the bike will do it for us anyway.

What could be more centred and harmonious than a spinning wheel?

11. The Brighton Roar

A 'roar' was an unofficial race arranged between clubs or within the club itself. Apparently such events were commonplace during the post-war period but were superseded as official road-racing became more and more widespread. We had all done our 'roaring' on clubruns and training nights. In the '50s the term was in everyday use, but as for the real thing, only the senior members had any direct experience.

By the middle of 1959 Bo, Ron Chitty and Den Blissett had all, for various reasons, stepped down from serious riding, and without their presence the clubrun had fallen into abeyance. I still popped round to see Bo on Sundays after I'd raced; he remained my coach and father figure, and it was he who came up with the idea of a roar. The old guard versus the new, a farewell and a renewal; it would be a friendly affair but with the usual resolute intent to test ourselves and each other. Why not a full-scale clubrun then? The notion took hold because we were all aware that we needed to acknowledge something momentous in its own small way: the passing of an era. This would be a special occasion which required a distancing from the familiar practices – deserved, in fact, a special ritual of its own. A lot of the things which in the normal run were likely to remain unsaid would be taken care of by the very form of the ritual. So it was that, like duellists or combatants in a friendly match, we met on neutral ground – beneath the decorative glass sign of the Reliable Fish Caterers on the corner of Becklow Road, already a place of historical significance because it used to serve as a winning post for sprint finishes.

I can describe the scene in detail because I've still got the commemorative snapshot. There we all are, lined up as convention demanded, all except Ron Chitty who, with typical bolshiness, is refusing to pose while still commanding the centre stage to pump up his tyres, his back turned to the camera. Blissett's bike stands at the kerb beside him, predictably mudguarded. We are all ranged behind a fence, wearing racing vests except for Blissett, the arch conservative again, who has managed only an ordinary white shirt. Bo stands out, equally true to his nature as a man ahead of his time, because he has donned racing shorts, the logical choice. None of the rest of us are quite so daring, settling for the lightweight bags we wore for clubruns. Blissett, of course, is sporting the more substantial whipcord variety. At that time racing shorts, even the thick woollen ones currently available, were judged too risqué for ordinary wear. In some cases our jerseys are covered by a slipover and thus disguised; a decade would pass before racing kit came fully out of the closet. I am standing skinny-legged and bashful on the right beside Blaise. Alan is off at the far left, in profile above Ron Chitty, seemingly addressing some remark across the group. The unseen cameraman is our only gesture to the formalities of the supposed duel; he is Bo's brother Ron who will act as our token second and motorcycle escort.

For all our outward composure, there is a certain nervousness in the air, some are obviously preoccupied, perhaps with how the day will progress and with their own comportment. In the up-and-coming camp there was no need to dwell on tactics, our strategy was ruthlessly straightforward: as we were all race fit, we need only attack from the word go and wind the others into an early submission. We were quietly confident; the real matter for deliberation was which one of us was going to win. My own plot to steal the honours had gone into operation earlier that morning. I'd prepared myself a steak breakfast like the Tour riders habitually devoured. But unused to anything more complicated than putting on the kettle and wary of the traditional rare version, I had reduced my bit of sirloin to a charred mass which I resolutely chomped through after my cornflakes. I was probably already feeling a little bilious.

We promenaded to the foot of Putney Hill in gentlemanly fashion, but once engaged upon the slopes I took the initiative to launch a blistering attack only to discover that my carbonised steak had come up to lodge itself in the middle of my chest where it was to stay for the rest of the day.

Our elders managed to stick to our wheels over the top, mainly because we were as winded as they were. All across Wimbledon Common and through the town we kept the pace high, the three of us relaying each on the front, but the others were coming through to break up our rhythm. On the hill out of Morden we renewed the attack, but the sly old foxes were still parrying our thrusts. At the front, I began to get impatient with these spoiling tactics and when I saw Ron Chitty coming through to break up our sequence once again, I tried to chop him off Alan's wheel. He was, of course, outraged by this breach of etiquette and fended me off with a hefty elbow plus a mouthful of abuse. We were already having a tougher time than expected.

It came out later that Blaise was meanwhile employing a more devious riposte to these manoeuvres. He sat at the back with Bo on his wheel, and as the long drag up to Epsom Downs began to bite, he fell back with Bo still behind him. Towards the top, when a significant gap had opened up, he simply jumped away and left our ever-generous guide and mentor floundering, condemned to a solo ride for the remainder of the journey.

At the front we were all a bit hammered by the fierceness of the opening exchanges; most of us were sitting in, waiting for our second wind.

It was then, coming out of the tree-lined undulations around Kingswood Manor, that Alan, ignoring the general ceasefire, squeezed himself away on the kerbside, his long, stringy legs cranking the pedals round with pigeon-toed laboriousness, his dry old chain and jockey wheels squeaking their protestations. But it was more than any of us could match and the gap widened inexorably. He was going away on his own. We were stunned by his energy and daring; all we could do was sit there and watch him disappear in the direction of Reigate and the long swoop down the hill. Ron Boxall on the motorcycle was the only one able to respond, he accelerated by to keep tabs on this startling development, while the four of us left settled into a bemused non-aggressive pact. The veterans were blown while Blaise and I willingly upheld the role of loyal teammates to our man up the road.

After Reigate, Ron gave us a time check across Hookwood Common and Alan was already a minute up. But this stirred nobody to action though it was obvious that he was pulling away. All competitiveness had been wrung from us, no one could face up to a similar effort. We trundled on across Gatwick airport and around the Crawley bypass until we hit the hill to Pease Pottage. Here Blaise roused himself to action,

'Come on,' he said to me, 'we can't just let him have it on a plate,' and jumped away. I had no alternative but to follow, though I was still trying to get my stomach to accept the morning's steak. We dropped the others with ease and began working together smoothly. But the long climbs of Handcross and Bolney began to sap me and before long I was doing shorter and shorter turns on the front. Up the long, curving incline towards Pyecombe, within striking distance of home, I was just hanging on. All at once Blaise turned and excitedly pointed towards the horizon. There was the stark, spindly figure of our prey still making the same rather laboured progress. Blaise took off in the blink of an eye. I was shot in legs and lungs and had to struggle over the last few bumps as best I could before cresting the long plunge down to the Brighton sign. I saw nothing of the chase or its outcome, but Alan had held on to secure the victory. His was by far the ride of the day, fulfilling the promise of the night he left us across Heathrow airport. Blissett came in the best of the old guard, from Ron Chitty and then Bo. We were all red-faced and windblown from our efforts and were glad of a sit-down on the grassy bank.

There was no great celebration of Alan's triumph. Each one of us muttered a few stock phrases, but really his exploit had left us almost speechless. We honoured it with that deference which would allow it to grow into a talking point for years to come.

Later, we pottered off into town to enjoy the delights of the seafront. At some point the younger generation decided that we would spend the afternoon on the beach and make our way home by train while our elders threw their legs over saddles to retrace the course of the roar. As Ron Chitty was to remark later: 'We were the real victors because we rode home.' And that casual parting marked the end of a golden era of club life for all of us.

When my stint at the factory came to an end I followed in the tyre marks of Bo and Ron Chitty by getting a job at Richmond Park golf course. After the rigours of J. Lyons, I spent the heatwave of September 'watering the gree-uns' as the Geordie head greenkeeper called them. All I had to do was play a hose on the carefully nurtured turf and watch out for flying golf balls. Those greens were pampered like prize show animals. Early in the morning we would all stride out carrying a 15-foot bamboo with a thinner beanstick wired to its end, to sweep the dew off the grass so that nothing but friction and gravity would impede the first putts. 'Rodding the greens' it was called; and as we set off into the dawn mist, shouldering our ancient poles, it was as if we were going forth to engage in some Biblical labour.

I did my cycling to and fro through a hard winter. Often the weather was so bad that we didn't stir from the tearoom – which suited my bookish ways perfectly. I was reading Camus and Sartre, broadening my knowledge of French literature and culture in general. I had embarked upon what nowadays is called a gap year; I was on my way to university. In the spring I would start making applications. There was a complication, however: in order to do a language course in those days you had to have O level Latin which I was without. Half-hearted efforts had been made in my last year to remedy this lack, but never enough to prepare me for an exam. I therefore began evening classes in the newly built Holland Park Comprehensive.

I worked on at the golf course until the spring of 1960 when I got fed up and left. My next employment was as a builder's labourer on the site of the new Shell-Mex building which was going up near Blackfriar's Bridge. This was an inconvenient ride with nowhere safe to park a bike so I went by Tube. It was a skivey sort of job, the site was huge and often there was little to do. My colleagues were rough-and-ready Irishmen who brought in their sandwiches wrapped in newspaper – we didn't have a lot in common. The days felt long with nearly an hour each end commuting so when somebody offered me a motorbike for twenty-five pounds, I invested without a qualm. It was an old Francis Barnet 125, but in running order – all I had to do was tax and insure it, get a provisional licence, put my L-plates up and I was on the road. I wasn't renouncing cycling, just providing myself with a convenient means of travelling to work.

There were various mishaps learning to ride it, mainly because I had no one to call on for help. One day the throttle jammed open while I was turning a corner – luckily in a side street – and I mounted the opposite pavement to crash into the wire cage protecting a sapling which left an imprint on my face. The poor tree was bent over at an angle of 45 degrees. I was so worried that I might be apprehended for malicious damage to council property that I made haste to leave the scene of the crime. The motorbike had stalled so rather than hang about I attempted a running start. The only trouble was that the impact had also dislodged the sole of my chukka boot and my efforts were hampered by a flapping tongue of rubber. Progress to competence was punctuated by such mishaps, but I survived and eventually became a regular motor-borne commuter.

One morning I reached my usual parking space on the South Bank but at the last moment I couldn't face work. On a sudden impulse I set out for Brighton.

By this time the experience of riding a motorbike had had a profound effect upon me. I was entranced by its effortlessness and ease; overnight I had become a convert to assisted motion. The power I had worked for so hard and so diligently before was now available at a twist of my wrist, and in an abundance that my legs could never match. It was an amazing discovery and a regular thrill which threw into question all the drudgery and striving of the previous years – in fact it made a nonsense of them. My old way of life suddenly seemed like a servitude to backward mechanics and narrow horizons. I was lifted free of a whole slew of accepted notions and burdensome habits. Who would ride a push-bike when you could have an engine between your knees? It seemed incredible that I had been hobbled by such wilful ignorance for so long. The feeling of freedom and release was intoxicating. I knew, of course, that from my former viewpoint I was betraying the true faith, that I was a turncoat and a heretic, but the possibility of guilt was laughable. I relished my about-face because it derived from liberation and joy. I threw my arms wide open to it since it was bigger than the little ideas that I had previously embraced. And this sense of jubilation lay behind my choice of Brighton that weekday morning, I was seizing the opportunity to rectify history, to symbolically renounce all my teenage pieties at a stroke. I was going for a joyride on those roads which represented duty and dedication, those miles that had once caused me so much hardship and false hope. I would revenge myself on them, gleefully profane their sacred ramps; mock those spirits of place, those deities of aspiration enshrined in tar and grit. I would bruise their sad old mugs with my great fat motor-driven tyres.

This sense of purpose and inspiration lasted until a few miles on the open road had passed and I began to feel a nagging chill which increased so that I was soon numb to the bone. Beyond

BIKE

a certain level of frigidity, I lost all possession of the ability to make a decision. I just sat there slowly turning to ice. Any other motivation was simply frozen out of me. But for arriving at Brighton, I might have chugged on until I succumbed to hypothermia. My whole trip down had been a fearful introduction to the main drawback of motorcycle travel. However many hot drinks I poured down myself on the desolate seafront, I could not thaw out – a fact which made the return journey almost a suicidal prospect. In my reduced state I was paralysed by dread and yet drawn to home as the only possible source of warmth. Eventually, I had no choice but to take to the road, promising myself to stop regularly for a warm-up. The whole jaunt had become like a day-trip to the Arctic in the clothes you stood up in. Even the draughty heights of the South Bank site seemed like a tropical paradise in comparison. By the evening my grand passion for motorcycling had been frozen out.

The labouring job got more and more boring. I tried to kill time by keeping a paperback in my pocket and hiding away to read, but that proved equally futile. Even the best of the Beat Generation could not block out my dismal circumstances. Then a nail went through the flimsy rubber of the inappropriate shoes I was wearing and I was carted off to hospital. I went back after my foot had healed, but that taste of leisure and freedom tipped the balance. My Latin exam was looming on the horizon. What little study I had managed over the winter would not be enough to see me through, I needed to go at it full-time. But I still had to work. In the small ads I found a paper round in the West End which suited me perfectly, I could get there in half an hour and be finished by 9.30 a.m. The shop was in amongst the art galleries off Piccadilly which were, in fact, our best customers. Afterwards I would have breakfast in my beloved Old Compton Street – a cappuccino and a rum baba in Sam Widges which was a small, narrow place with high-backed benches and a bar, an old-fashioned coffee house. I usually sat at the bar like an habitué. Once my morning treat was over I would repair to Westminster library and get out my books.

This idyll was interrupted one bright, sunny morning when, rattling up Piccadilly towards Green Park station, an old lady jumped off the kerb straight into my path. I was faced with the decision either to kill her on the spot or throw myself round her. I did the honourable thing and the next I knew I was in a high-ceilinged room lying on a slab. My right chukka boot seemed to be pointing off at an odd angle and I felt a certain looseness in my connection with it; further than that I was disinclined to investigate. I had broken my leg – a nasty fracture of both tibia and fibula which had to be secured by several screws.

For the next three weeks I spent a very pleasant time in a ward of St George's Hospital at Hyde Park Corner among men and boys in much the same predicament. We weren't really ill, just temporarily disabled so spirits were high; on top of which we were fussed over by a succession of young nurses who obviously enjoyed the male company.

I had a stream of visitors during the long summer evenings, including Blaise and Alan just back from a touring holiday in France. They had used it as preparation for the big event of the club's season, the Chequers Grand Prix. So, dutifully on the appropriate Monday morning, I stopped the man who brought the papers round and bought a *Daily Telegraph* to look up the result. There at the bottom of the page, amongst a little end-of-column ragbag of club events was a single name against the heavier black type of the race title – it was A. Hawkins (Chequers).

I was stunned. A whole welter of emotions swept over me beginning with surprise and disbelief. How had he managed it after revealing that Blaise had given him a hard time climbing in the Alps? Out in the Chilterns there was hardly a level mile. He was a giraffe rather than a mountain goat, yet he had won a climber's race. It was inexplicable, but however many times I looked at the paper the tiny letters returned the same verdict.

But this quibbling with detail was only a holding operation while the real emotional backlash built into a great wave. The next few moments were to be my introduction to that galling potion we all must swallow at some time during our lives: the unexpected success of friends. A huge breaker whisked me up and flung me back sprawling onto my bed. Why did he have to do this to me now, just when any such prospects had been severed with my shin bones? What was wrong with the cosy anonymity we both shared? Why didn't he have the good grace to just plod on like the rest of us? Then there was the bitter realisation of just how close it had been – a new season, a foreign tour; it might have been me – which led to the further discovery that beneath all the facile excuses and the motorcycle madness, my heart still yearned to do what he had done. My plight, which had been hitherto quite bearable, was now a torture. It was too much, too unjust; I was suddenly close to tears.

By the time Alan came in looking lean and radiant that evening, I had collected myself sufficiently to congratulate him warmly. He was modestly offhand about the whole thing, explaining that he had ridden away at the halfway stage and they had never caught him. Any trace of my self-pitying tantrums of the morning were firmly dispelled by his good-natured friendliness. How could I not be happy for him when he allowed me to enjoy, even only by proxy, something that we had all aspired to?

Of course the imminence of the Latin exam, so crucial to my future, had been pushed aside by the orthopaedic emergency and totally ignored in the holiday camp atmosphere of the ward. I just fervently prayed that I would still be in hospital at the fatal hour and thus have a good excuse for missing it. No such luck – I was discharged on crutches with two days to spare. A gung-ho hero would have struggled in nonetheless, but I knew that I was utterly unprepared. All I could do was write a tear-stained letter to Birmingham explaining the circumstances and regretfully withdrawing my application until the next intake. I had resigned myself to filling in for another year when a quick return of post arrived welcoming me anyway, as long as I kept up my studies of the dead language. This revived my spirits completely and though my cycling career seemed at an end, I was back on the bike sooner than expected. Once the plaster came off I found riding far easier than walking, and was encouraged by the hospital to use it as a means of re-education – another ironic turn of the wheel.

12. Cycling as Art

The bicycle has always fascinated artists – even perhaps before the fact. One of the greatest of them all, Leonardo da Vinci, is credited with a sketch of a prototype two-wheeled vehicle, and he certainly did good work on the chain.

Maurice Vlaminck, a prominent Post Impressionist, is reputed to have been a professional racing cyclist before he turned to brush and canvas. He might well be an ancestor of Roger (Monsieur Paris–Roubaix) De Vlaeminck, an artiste in another medium. The Cubist Georges Braque was a keen cyclist and put his bike into a famous work, but due to the demands of the genre, it is hardly discernible. His friend and rival, Picasso, fashioned a notable visual pun by arranging a saddle and a pair of handlebars into a bull's head. But the most striking and influential appropriation of the bike occurred when Marcel Duchamp took a front wheel on a pair of forks and mounted them on a stool as a pleasing object of contemplation. This whimsical impulse developed into a whole philosophy of art – the ready-made which the artist endorses by his choice – that is still being pursued today by young firebrands of the avant-garde. Duchamp found repose in watching the spokes vanish and then re-appear as the wheel slowed down. He found that it took his mind off everyday concerns and opened up other perspectives. The spinning wheel was a comforting presence, a source of reverie, like watching a fire dance in a grate.

Aren't Londoners deriving the same consolation from the Millennium Wheel? Most commentators have agreed that it resembles nothing so much as a giant bicycle wheel. Maybe

107

it's a sign that the capital will become again a cycling city.

In the '70s there was a painting of a Mercier *Course Professionnelle* silhouetted against a dawn sky which was much reproduced in cycling magazines. It was an effort to establish the racing bike as an art object, which of course it is. I don't know about today's grotesques with their bulbous tubes and fat wheels, but certainly the top-notch bikes of that era had a classical purity of line and form which elevated them well above the merely utilitarian.

There is, however, a contemporary British artist who has sought to express the far more interesting effects of bicycle culture on the individual psyche. He is Anthony Green, a noted Royal Academician who hangs several paintings every year in the Summer Exhibition as well as holding regular shows both in this country and as far away as Japan. He has used his youthful obsession with continental road racing as inspiration for a series of witty and pointed observations of his own reactions to the sport.

He freely admits that his pictures are largely fantasy and his forthrightness confronts us with the truth: what he has recorded is nothing more than what we have all felt at one time or another – those leaps of the imagination which install us in the yellow jersey, for instance, or allow us to pull off a win in the World Championship.

One of his earlier works is a conventional head-and-shoulders self-portrait except that he is wearing the famous race leader's emblem, and is called simply *Maillot Jaune*. But with *Le Pistard* ('The Trackman') and other paintings he has used the same self-revelation to more complex ends. In essence he holds up a mirror to his own enthusiasm and gives us a picture of that peculiar beast, the cycling fan.

To come upon such pictures on a gallery wall is to experience that thrill of recognition which greets a kindred spirit. 'I'm not quite as cracked as I thought I was,' you tell yourself and smile in gratitude to Green for having the perception and wit to put it all up there.

He caught the bug early, and at the source. His mother is French and she took him home for holidays regularly after the end of the War. And so, on one high-summer afternoon in his eighth year, revelation burst upon him:

> We were sitting under the shade of a tree in a café by the roadside and these nut-brown men in coloured jerseys came rushing by. Some of them threw their bikes on the ground and tried to get water to fill up their bottles. There was a fountain and I remember them plunging their heads right up to the shoulders, they'd got tyres round them.
>
> It was like a science fiction film. From not knowing it was even a possibility, suddenly it was there, shooting past – the Tour de France. It was quite overwhelming.

So overwhelming that to this day some of his trackmen turn up with a spare tyre knotted around their shoulders.

His split nationality gives him that privileged access to both sides of the Channel that we all aspire to. Some kind of divided loyalty is inevitable for the enthusiast in this country; we are all exiles looking on from beyond the boundaries of the real action. Imagine a keen cricketer living out his life in France. We are constantly either abetting invasion or trying to import the special *ambiance* of the continental scene. The demise of the Prutour is the latest in a long line of attempts to graft that capricious vine for home consumption.

Le Pistard, a large semi-circular self-portrait along the lines of *Maillot Jaune* but with much more detail, shows a crash-hatted Green against a Six Day backdrop. He is riding for Britain as the Union Jacks on his shoulders signify, but in his gold-rimmed glasses (a distinctly French pair) there is a reflection in each lens of identical sprinters: one in French, one in British colours, presumably dead-heating. It is a picture about divided loyalties, but not just nationality. Although he is riding for his country, the logo across his chest spells out a subsidiary sponsor: 'Mary', his wife. It is she who looks on from the track bridge in the background, on one side holding a wheel and on the other a frame. She is an ever-present mechanic, *soigneur* and general supporter. Green's expression is soberly decisive, facing up to the challenge of the evening's chases.

When I went to see the artist in his studio, he eagerly recounted the development of his enthusiasm.

> My French relatives were very cynical about it all. They kept saying: 'Well of course, nowadays it's bent. Before the War it was straight, men won on merit.' I used to pooh-pooh this and I still think that anybody who could climb over two mountain ranges and get to Paris first was something special – even with the doping scandals.
>
> When I lecture now and show the cycling slides, I ask the students: doesn't it capture your imagination? You get to the top of a mountain and you have to stuff newspapers down your jersey to descend the other side – one minute you're boiling hot and the next you're on the verge of pulmonary congestion. You're almost fighting each other off, trying to stick your pump in the other bloke's wheel. I find it fascinating myself.

When Bobet began winning Tours in the mid-'50s, Green decided, like the rest of us, that what he must have was a Louison Bobet special. But unlike the rest of us he was able, through the French connection, to have a frame shipped over.

'It was all done out in yellow with blue transfers and a picture of the man himself on the seat tube. For the time it was a very flashy bicycle. I got Ted Gerrard up in Finchley to put it together for me and – surprise, surprise, I've still got it.'

Indeed there is a shot of Green riding it in two of the three BBC2 documentaries about his career.

It is appropriate then, that most of Green's cycling pictures bear French titles, the only exceptions being those which comment on that more universal mode of expression, love. There is an element of this even in *Le Pistard* what with the omnipresence of his wife. In other pictures she becomes the beauty queen and even the fruits of victory (see *L'Equipe*).

She is integral to his art and also to his cycling.

> The first picture that I painted with a cycling theme is of me in a tracksuit and Italian racing socks with my beloved Louison Bobet, standing in the foothills of the Pyrenees with Mary next to me.
>
> Most of my painting is based upon family life, marriage, and the implication was that here was the man who had everything: the beautiful girl, the beautiful bike, the beautiful mountains in the background.

But things can't stay frozen for ever, he must somehow justify this bounty, he must live up to her expectations. He must leave off just holding the bike and move into the foreground as a champion cyclist, a hero.

'I see the artist as a sort of hero figure in a non-heroic age. People say it's unheroic because we're not in the middle of World War II, but you have to look for the heroic in the age you're in. And on a quieter, smaller level just trying to do a good job is a kind of heroism.'

Traditionally, the sport has always offered an opportunity for those of humble origins to rise in the world, so the image is a potent one. On the other hand, it is a bit of a joke, a wish-fulfilment fantasy. But Green is not content to let the matter be passed off lightly. He says:

> The artist and the cyclist have the same problems. In the case of the cyclist it's a special gift to be able to ride fast over long distances, to go through suffering, have the character to hang on when others pack. It's the same with the artist. You need the talent to begin with, but you've also got to be able to go on painting when you're

being ignored. And just like the cyclist you can actually
burn yourself out.

I've earned my living at it for some years which in
itself is as difficult as earning a living riding a bicycle –
and just as chancy. I never know from one year to the
next whether, in fact, I'm going to be able to carry on.

So the artist throws away his traditional beret and depicts
himself as a crash-hatted gladiator. In *Champions* Green
celebrates himself in various guises: as a motor-paced daredevil
and eventually, larger than life, as an old fashioned *routier*. We
are back among the nut-brown Tour men, the first heroes.

In *Souvenir of Adolescence*, Mary has moved into the
foreground, she is now the dominant element. We are in the
room where Green places a lot of his work, his studio – again
that self-referential starting point. It stands for the basic,
unchanging consciousness perhaps, the inside of his head.

Cycling is one of the passions of adolescence, but it must
give way to the more basic drive of sex. The strutting,
provocative pin-up is brought to life on home ground. Who
better to portray her but Mary, just to keep it in the family. Yet
there is no hint of a sanctified relationship. She is giving him
the eye, but our hero is significantly riding for himself this
time, his sponsor's logo proclaims it: 'Green'. He is sitting at a
table strewn with bike parts, his eyes glazed over.

They are re-visiting the passionate world of unrequited desire
– the very core of adolescence – playing out this remembrance
of what seemed so far away then, but is now within easy reach.
We are in the realm of clothes fetishism: Dad's in his cycling
gear and Mum's in her hot-pants.

'You see yourself as a champion cyclist, but you also see your
wife as Brigitte Bardot. She's got to have the right outfit on. If
it's clogs and sacking it wouldn't be the same thing.'

Mary's long, slender legs are the eye-catching centre of the
picture; combining sleek allure with fine musculature, they
straddle the twin obsessions of pedalling and coupling.

Anthony Green's track-mitted left hand is resting on the table, but the right is hidden underneath; presumably, given the circumstances, otherwise engaged.

In the years of Green's adolescence – and mine – racing gear was the sacramental robe of a persecuted sect; it could only be worn publicly in the presence of a full complement of similarly dressed initiates. You were the hapless victim of a paradoxical divide. Across the Channel the racing cyclist was a respected member of the community; he lined up with the town's dignitaries: the mayor, the priest, the huntsman and all the other honest burghers, in his tight black shorts and jersey. In this country, on the other hand, the same garb would make you the object of blank-faced suspicion, that silent disapproval which is more powerful than abuse – and you would get that too.

The free display of the most practical wear for the enjoyment of your chosen sport was frowned upon – it just wasn't done. Mind you, no one ran around the streets in skimpy running shorts either. Now, of course, you can bomb about like a Mapei superstar and nobody turns a hair. Old men of the '50s and '60s have long since come out of their closets to relish the consummation they so devoutly wished for in their youth – but that was where you did your posing then, behind closed doors. And this is what *Souvenir of Adolescence* also touches upon: the emblematic charge of that suit of lights, the almost sexual pleasure there was to be had in wearing it.

In *L'Equipe* we are in the same room, with the same couple, but things are altogether different. There is a spare, concentrated tension about *Souvenir of Adolescence* which is in keeping with its subject. It depicts the pressure of self-involvement which persists until action is called for – the commitment of the adult world.

In *L'Equipe* we are in that world, all bustle and movement; the adults themselves are the centre of it. What they are celebrating here is not desire, but its end result: a happy marriage. The partners are the 'team' of the title, a madison

113

pair; life is a Six Day. The track has taken over their living room.

They are making a change, a symbolic passing-on, a gesture of love: he is giving her a gold bangle. Mary is the recipient now, the passive one and Green is the humble plaintiff in his training gear.

The room itself, no longer the bare backcloth, now shares a starring role. A crank and a shoe-plate on the floor, an old Huret changer on the mantlepiece – every enthusiast must recognise the scene. The chairs are stand-ins for bikes. 'I used that chair because it's made of tubular steel,' he told me, 'seems like the nearest thing to a bicycle you have in the house.'

Hers is the racer, but his is a more comfortably upholstered model. In the old Sixes which required longer hours of the riders, they would circle the track at their ease between sessions – this is the mood of the piece.

The spectators by the trackside are the artist again in various guises: as another rider goggled up for a motor-paced event and as a Union Jack-vested competitor – both references to companion pictures.

In *L'Equipe* Green has gathered together most of the themes he has dealt with in his cycling work and brought them to their most pointed expression. It is his most witty and concentrated version of mature love in a cycling context; it is the eternal duet played to a chorus of pounding boards and whirring silks; it is Adam and Eve in the *Vélodrome d'Hiver*.

There are very few standards of comparison for the cycling artist – and indeed, Anthony Green stands virtually alone. We have to go back across the Channel to find a figure who is in any way as distinct and commanding – and that in a different form.

Anyone who remembers the old Tour magazines will also recall the teeming panoramas drawn by Pellos, the cartoonist. He did brilliant, instantly recognisable caricatures of all the leading personalities and placed them in a landscape which also had a face – the mountains, the milestones, everything was somehow humanised.

With Green, the focus is more personal but the vision is equally distinct, the realisation as masterful. There is the same sweep of the imagination into unforeseen dimensions, but above all, the same humour, the same delight in the foibles and grandeurs of that peculiar conjunction of man and machine which is cycling.

Without doubt the greatest work of art to come out of cycling thus far is Jorgen Leth's *A Sunday in Hell*. It purports to be a documentary about Paris–Roubaix, but in reality it is a sustained hymn of praise to riding a bike and in particular to that exalted pitch of competitive effort in which nothing is held back and no concession made. All the rest is a tease, delaying tactics to sharpen our senses for the finale. Sean Kelly was reputed to be able to make love to the cobbles. Leth puts that experience up on the silver screen, but it is more like a rape, with those relentless stones as rapist.

We start with the mundane business of cleaning a bike. A Sanson mechanic brushes away at a team machine – Moser's perhaps – briskly adjusting a brake caliper with the shaft of a hammer and checking the gears. The sequence progresses without any sound other than the clanking and chattering of moving parts. Then, just as the whole business is about to go on too long, the solemn notes of a cello break the silence, alerting us to the fact that we are witnessing something important. That this pitiful skeleton, wheel-less and hung in the air, worthy only of brusque manhandling, is the key to a great drama which is about to unfold. The whole protracted introduction is a quiet fanfare for the marvellous use man has made of the humble bicycle. Leth will elaborate his case with vivid camera-work and inspired editing, but also by continuously plying us with similar emotional prompts. He marshals his sounds as meticulously as he does his pictures.

He is always aware that a rider on a bike must be complemented with the swish of tyres on tarmac, the singing of a transmission – it is a characteristic of all his films. He knows, as a bike rider himself, that those almost subliminal effects snare us into complete identification, we are in there turning those pedals. But these are just flourishes compared to the bravura of his most striking innovation: commissioning a special score of musical themes and motifs to enhance and counterpoint the action. At a stroke he lifts the depiction of cycle sport from the lower reaches of tinkling whimsy. The mood of the film, dictated by the first cello solo, is intense, celebratory, even elegaic. What the music is not is the frothy, whirligig stuff that usually accompanies any screen-portrayal of pushing of the pedals.

Leth approaches the race with an unprecedented level of respect and by sounding that note so powerfully and by showing it so vividly he draws that same level from the viewer. He makes us realise what we have always felt: that love of the sport which goes even beyond respect, probably to awe. This old hallowed ritual, a regular feast-day in the cycling calendar since 1896 is, for the first time, accorded its true weight and resonance on film.

After the stars are shown gathering at their hotels and preparing for action, we get a brutal foretaste of what this action might entail. Black and white footage reveals the worst passages from a previous year, and the soundtrack rams home the message with an emphatic pounding on the kettle drums. This is martial music, the sound of battle fiercely engaged – of which we will hear much more when the race hits the cobbles.

During the early miles of peaceful promenading along tree-lined *Routes Nationales*, the Paris–Roubaix theme, introduced by the cello, is picked up by a male-voice choir in a deep resonant bass and expands into a plainsong anthem like a secular Gregorian Chant only to be suddenly interrupted by a crash. (These sudden shifts of mood and tempo are another directorial device in that they mimic the rhythm of the race itself.) When the field reconvenes, the plainsong builds to a rapturous climax. Here we have the race as colourful spectacle, all competitiveness laid aside in the sheer enjoyment of skimming along through the spring sunshine. As a lyrical statement of the joys of cycling its only peer is the title sequence from Truffaut's first film, *Les Mistons*, in which we see a pretty girl in a billowing skirt pedalling barefoot out to the hills around Nîmes for a rendezvous with her boyfriend.

The race is the driving narrative, but Leth also weaves in some fascinating sidelights on the life of a pro bike rider: Merckx's pernicketiness with his machine, for instance; how his senior lieutenant had the privilege of adjusting the master's handlebar and saddle height; the kind of reception awaiting in the broom wagon; how a mishap can leave riders without a feed; the protocol of the podium and what to expect in the showers afterwards. He also establishes the social and economic background to the whole enterprise. The demonstration plays into his hands on this count since it serves to emphasise just how central Paris–Roubaix is to the popular consciousness. The printers want to make the headlines but they are careful only to interfere with the early stages where no great harm will be done. Paris–Roubaix is a sure-fire attention grabber, but it is also a sporting monument, too prestigious to really mess up. The men are notably deferential to the riders, even fawning upon the stars. Only the women are unsporting enough to harangue *les coureurs*. The prominence given to Eurovision underlines the sport's appeal as a media commodity all over the Continent, and thus its commercial viability.

While the general picture is being deftly brushed in, the race is gradually accelerating. At Valenciennes we see the bunch coming through at a blistering pace, a fact which is emphasised by the frantic klaxoning and the way that the static camera lingers on the whole caravan with its foot down trying to keep up. We next find Talbourdet on his own at Neuvilly, and then as he is first onto the cobbles. He is going well until the hill stiffens and this sets the scene for one of the most exciting sequences in the whole film. De Vlaeminck suddenly pops up among the following motorcycles and surges past. Cue a skittish cello and then the kettle drums as Roger forges on. We cut to the panic among the stragglers. Then to Maertens and Dierickx as they catch De Vlaeminck in slow motion with loud drumbeats. Long-shot of dusty roads snaking between the folds of green fields. A leading group has formed, and half a minute behind is a chasing group led by Merckx. We backtrack then to see stragglers and puncture victims, the havoc that has been caused by De Vlaeminck's offensive. Then we return to the main bunch and dwell on the valiant other ranks as they labour to keep up. Slow motion against a heaving rendition of the Paris–Roubaix theme seems to merge them into any of mankind's fabled endeavours. They could well be the Argonauts rowing forth in quest of the Golden Fleece or some Roman slaves hauling limestone blocks to build the Colosseum. Even the team cars as they loom through the dust, men perched upon them intently scanning the far distance, take on this timeless air. They could be charioteers on some ancient Greek plain searching for the enemy. By inspired manipulation, Leth makes us feel how such an event fulfils our deep and perennial hunger for the grand scale, the epic.

The whole first part of the film has been a preparation for this climax and now we take a breather out in the country on a cobbled bend. Leth begins to elaborate a second movement: Freddy Maertens' desperate chase and the skirmishes which lead to the winning break.

De Vlaeminck sends De Muynck and Osler up the road and Merckx strings out the leading group in pursuit. At this point we begin to hear again that high, ringing tone which is the aural equivalent of a red alert. It is never that intrusive because it chimes in perfectly with the tenor of events, but Leth just tweaks up the emotional volume in all the subsequent action scenes.

Merckx is still chasing. What is never disclosed in the film is the fact that the Cannibal suffered nine stoppages due to punctures or mechanical trouble. Normal mortals are condemned by just a couple. Yet he is always at the head of affairs wherever he finds himself. His usual style is to *mener un train d'enfer* as the French say – to set a hellish pace – and the phrase is never so apt as it is to his riding over the cobbles.

Inbetween times we see some crash victims, a terrible gash for the unfortunate Jobo rider and an anguished wheel-change for Poulidor. Sibille tries a lone break from the leading group. Again there are bodies strewn across the road like casualties on a real battlefield. Plankaert, one of the favourites, has forfeited his chance.

There follows a series of video inserts of unremitting aggression as De Vlaeminck tries to tear the legs off Maertens and Moser. All the stragglers, including Godefroot and Raas, have to claw their way back just to remain in contention. It is sublime madness, racing at fever pitch, a glimpse of these old cobbled tracks transformed into an inferno. Only the most durable will stand the heat.

Then Maertens crashes and retires. Godefroot shows he is no flat-foot on the bumps and gets the slo'-mo' treatment to endorse his tag as the Bulldog of Flanders. Our canine bruiser subsequently gets into the winning break with De Vlaeminck, De Meyer and Kuiper, only to puncture, but he justifies his cameo later by an explosive sprint off the banking to put lengths into Merckx and the other also-rans. If he had been allowed to stay with the break what might he not have done? Two years later he was able to win a Tour of Flanders from a similar group of youngsters.

Moser gets up from behind, scything through Poulidor and Danguillaume who just cannot close the gap. The break takes on its final shape with De Vlaeminck and Moser working and De Meyer and Kuiper sitting in. The cutting becomes more frantic as we include the TV vans and commentators sending out the last hour over the air. Kuiper attacks and is quickly sat upon. Back to Merckx and the chasers – they are now beaten men. Moser takes a flyer but Roger is as tireless as ever. Kuiper tries again with the same fate. They are now on the run-in to the track. Kuiper stretches his back and waggles his calves. Behind, Merckx has flung himself into a last effort but is caught. On the track De Vlaeminck leads out with disastrous results. The race is lost in the final straight to the wheel-sucker. Even Moser squeezes past him. Poor Roger is the day's biggest dupe to Hell's implacable caprice.

De Meyer shows no qualms, he has earned his victory by the only means at his disposal. A win in Paris–Roubaix is a win by any measure. On the podium, that old schemer, Guillaume Driessens, has a gleeful grin for his overwhelmed protégé.

Leth leaves us with a poignant endpiece. Like miners surfacing after a long shift at the coalface, the riders gather in their gloomy chapel of cleansing with its shoulder-high pews. Voluble now, where they were tight-lipped at the start, they intone their evensong to a congregation of newsmen. All the triumphs and the griefs, the satisfaction and the discontent spill out until we pan to the final redemptive image of Ole Ritter. He is the little-known soldier whose story no one waits upon so he is giving himself up to the consolations of the shower. His features, picked out by the soft light and deep shadow, are further transformed by the glistening water so that his becomes the triumphant head of everyman living to fight another day. At which point the cello takes up again those solemn notes of elegy, reminding us of where we first came in: with the equally humble bicycle.

It was not a great Paris–Roubaix – except that it has been captured for all time. The great editions show a hero triumphing against all odds: Dirk de Mol in '88, Duclos Lasalle in '92, Tchmil in '94. But they would have, perhaps, made a lesser film. The flawed version speaks more profoundly of the race's true nature. There is a kind of Shakespearean sweep to Leth's depiction. He shows it all and lets us understand it all; he catches the essence of a particular event so well that he gives us life itself. We recognise something of our own ongoing struggle in those stirring deeds, and we rejoice.

When I first saw the film at the National Film Theatre in 1979, you could feel the audience rising to the film well before the end. Here was proof at last that our grand passion was a worthy one. We were taken out of ourselves, justified and exalted at the same time. As soon as the lights went up we were all smiles, everyone was of the same accord. You felt like embracing your near neighbours – only real art can do that.

We all owe a debt of gratitude to Ray Pascoe for making this masterpiece available to the home audience.

The truth is that cycle racing at the highest level is itself an unacknowledged popular art form drawing upon elements of drama, ballet, circus and carnival parades set against a natural backdrop. Animated by speed and competitiveness, it has that sense of momentum and momentousness, of coming from afar and going on further, of conquering great difficulties which gives its brief passage the sweep of grandeur. Then there is the superhuman athleticism of the riders, their wholeheartedness, the sheer flair of their physical expressiveness individually and en masse. The whole spectacle, however experienced, is both thrilling and appeasing at the same time because it is a living demonstration of something eternal and ever-present: the higher reaches of life, the indomitable human spirit.

13. Epiphany in
Old Compton Street

At the beginning of the '60s, I put my teenage dreams and disappointments behind me and took up adult pursuits like drinking, and then latterly drinking and driving. My new-found university friends introduced me to the pleasures of Watney's Red Barrel which fired us up with lust for our female counterparts. After years of sober austerity, self-indulgence crooked her finger and I was led willingly astray.

Though I took my bike up to Birmingham in the autumn of 1960, I hardly touched it except for one Saturday night when two of us tried to ride it home – drunk of course – and we fell off on Moseley Hill to lie sprawled in the road laughing, heedless of any risk. But not a single car passed either way until our guffaws had run their course.

At the end of term, that former symbol of my high ideals, lately become a lowly workhorse, went home to see out the decade underneath a sheet of polythene against a garden wall.

Full-time study on a maximum grant (eighty pounds per term rising to a hundred) provided a life of comfort and excess. I had an adequate income, beer was a shilling (five pence) a pint, so was a meal in the refectory; lodgings were equally cheap. The work was stimulating and the social life was a whirl. But at the end of it I was dead keen to get back to the workaday world. In 1963, academia seemed fusty and at odds with the bustling promise of the blossoming '60s spirit. Most of us wanted to be out in the action, not stuck in a backwater. More than anything, I wanted a car – that was the key to the playboy lifestyle to which all of us young turks aspired.

Early in our undergraduate careers, Moss – a fellow Londoner – and I were hitching back from a weekend at home when we were picked up by a smoothie in something grand like a Rover. As we settled into the warm interior – the radio playing softly – and made the appropriate noises of gratitude and wonder, our host took his cue and began to sing the praises of the company car. How everything was taken care of, even a percentage of private mileage, how he cruised about virtually free of charge in this glamour wagon. 'It's the only way to run a car,' he counselled us smugly. Both of us were spellbound by the sweet smell of leather upholstery, the aura of the 'executive'. This was a word just gaining currency then, and we held it to our hearts with grubby student fingers while squirrelling away its open-sesame: the pharmaceutical industry.

But of course, when it came to the negotiating table in the Appointments Board, nobody wanted two lower-second arts graduates in the new dawn of British Business. They quickly spotted our lassitude and indifference born of three years of suiting ourselves and three months of feverish swotting before the final exams. We were no 'self-starters' however hard we acted up. All the grim industrial giants gave us the cold shoulder for their graduate entry schemes.

When all was lost – when the degree ceremony had come and gone, and in its wake more failed interviews; when all the chosen had long since departed into their dark, satanic mills, and with a new fresher's week about to pop over the horizon, Moss and I were still working as plumber's mates on the new physics block, clinging on where we were no longer wanted except in this hangdog capacity – we remembered again that glowing car ride and set our last desperate sights on peddling drugs.

Nothing happened until after Christmas which found us holed-up back in London. But then suddenly Moss went AWOL and reappeared after a fortnight with an Austin A40 – his ticket to ride, his company jam-jar. The swine had even taken the precaution of learning to drive years before.

It took the rest of the year, but by the autumn I too had my foot on the first rung of the executive ladder, I was a trainee medical representative.

The training course was a breeze, six weeks in a country hotel all found. Lessons nine-to-five and an exam on Friday afternoon – it was like being back at university again. But on the subsequent field training, with a particularly wooden example of the trade, I discovered the dreary round of doctor's surgeries and hospital waiting-rooms that the job entailed and my heart sank. I knew then that I would never make a go of it. Things looked up, however, when I was allotted Hampstead as my territory and on my first day I was able to join Moss for lunch at the Swiss Grill, the rep's watering hole. There I found that fiddling calls was a widespread practice and I began to put off till tomorrow what had already been put off till today.

Despite the undoubted trials that lay ahead, I had the consolation of a new Ford Cortina – instant position and status, the key to everything as far as I was concerned. The passion wagon, the booze-mobile was mine. At a moment's notice I could shoot off to the hostelry of choice and slurp the evening away with boon companions. Come last orders, I could root out a party, however far afield, and set off with my harem of birds and a six-pint can snug in the boot. I could swill and squire with the best.

But our antics were not as excessive as even we believed them to be. During the real ale revolution, it came to light that Red Barrel was so low in alcohol that it would have passed for near beer during Prohibition. No wonder it took three pints of the stuff to have any effect at all.

In 1965 we drove down to Spain in Moss's Hillman – he'd stepped up a notch. On the way we caught the finish of a Tour stage in the foothills of the Pyrenees. I saw a lot of familiar faces in the flesh for the first time – a sweaty, haggard flesh, no longer so formidable or so admirable. I even bought a magazine, but nothing connected in the old way which was hardly surprising since by that time I was a fat-arsed, beer-bellied, sedentary slob. My feet were accustomed to different pedals.

Although I had come top in the training course and high hopes were attached to my name, I never managed to do the job competently. But I survived because the business was booming, and in 1967 I jumped ship for another firm just ahead of the bullet. By the late '60s, though, my time was running out and I didn't care. One morning in November '69, my area manager and his sidekick arrived to repossess the Cortina, hot on the heels of a letter announcing my sudden death as an employee. I had been tipped off, but I ignored the warning, naively believing that they wouldn't sack me before Christmas.

All of a sudden I was back on the bike again. Luckily, I had exhumed it from the garden a year previously to make a short-lived comeback. I was probably thirteen stone at the time and found the whole thing a different proposition to what it had been when I weighed ten.

But what a shock it was to be without a car. My social life crumbled and a painful period of re-adjustment followed, cushioned to some extent by the dole and a budding romance.

I had to get on my bike in more senses than one, but any return to being a fully committed enthusiast proceeded only very gradually. What I didn't realise was that I was drawn by the spirit of the times. During the '70s, the profile of cycle sport began to rise in the public consciousness to a level it had not enjoyed since the glory days of Reg Harris in the '40s and early '50s. This occurred mainly through TV and under the impetus of another charismatic personality – Eddy Merckx.

One Saturday afternoon in the spring of '71, I was slumped in front of the box when a strange vision took over the screen – cycle racing. On a track strikingly reminiscent of Herne Hill on a damp Good Friday, a large road-man dressed mainly in black sat on the wheel of a much smaller rival. It was like watching a cat play with a mouse. The burden of inevitability weighed heavily on both as they put in the prescribed lap and a half; the mouse seemed resigned to his fate, and the cat was not moving a whisker unnecessarily. Sure enough, coming off the last banking, the cat pounced, swallowed up the mouse and swept across the line to victory. The commentator explained that Georges Pintens, the mouse, had done the ride of his life by catching the great Eddy Merckx for five minutes in the closing miles. This was my first glimpse of the rider who was to become the supreme champion of all time. Unfortunately I had caught him on one of his rare off-days. Little did I know then how much I would come to dote on such occasions and grow to love the spirited Walloon. The only hint of this development came from the mental note I made to keep an eye on Dicky Davies's *World of Sport*, especially around classic's time. My re-conversion was under way.

Later that year, as a result of my continued search for an agreeable niche in the workaday world, I found myself at a doorway in Wardour Street, on the borders of Soho. My host was Melvin, a previous colleague from the lower depths of BBC Publications, who had moved on to a rather shady magazine called *Curious* which promoted sex education for adults. All the way there he had roundly denounced the contents, the philosophy and the management of this enterprise – even his own role in it, which I gathered to be in mail order – but nonetheless, he had agreed to show me round as his prospective assistant. Such denunciations only served to make the place more intriguing and his own troubled conscience more apparent. He was preparing me for the worst, but I knew already that it was a far better bet than the dead-end I was presently inhabiting.

The offices were above a Chinese restaurant called the 'Lee Ho Fook', the appropriateness of which most newcomers felt moved to comment upon. As I rose to the bait, Melvin pretended not to hear and led me into a scruffy corridor then up a flight of stairs. The gloom darkened as we climbed. The walls were black and only a small sooty window high up shed any light. We reached a roomy landing and Melvin stepped forward to unlock a large door which released floods of light from the street into the stairwell.

'Abandon hope, all ye who enter here,' he intoned as he ushered me in.

In contrast to the gothic murk of the stairs, the walls inside were painted white. We did a tour of the various offices with Melvin damning each one's absent tenant until we went out the back to a pokier, L-shaped room where he dumped his bag on a desk. My own position was to be at the end of the stave of the L, tucked away between floor-to-ceiling shelving on one side and a narrow worktop on the other. The shelves were full of strange, rubber objects and weirdly contorted glassware like you would find in a surgical appliance shop window. These were the sex-aids which constituted a profitable spin-off from the sale of the magazine, providing a ready income, which according to Melvin, kept the whole show afloat. I sat down at the worktop with its litter of Jiffy bags and postage machine and felt immediately at home. Perhaps in this peculiar environment with its disreputable merchandise I might fit in and prosper.

Starting work the next week was like joining the cast of one of the more risqué Whitehall farces which were a staple of the West End theatre of the time. The accountant, a trendy young buck forever pitched forward by built-up heels, spent his day snapping polaroids of prospective nude models. A regular ad in *Time Out* kept him amply supplied. But although he maintained a neat file of all the applicants, the art department never used them as a matter of principle – he was seen to be trespassing on their territory. The editor, an Oxford man gone pop, with a hairy chest and medallion, would often find it necessary to leave his work in order to make the waiting girls feel at home. And should there be any polaroiding in progress, he would invariably need a contemplative stroll towards the studio doorway. When Gerald, the boss, came in he, too, would join in the sport.

The whole, often frantic, business of the outer office revolved around this totally redundant activity. Only the art department held themselves aloof, their door remained firmly closed. They were fierce young aesthetes fresh out of art school who despised the 'tit-and-bum' policy which Gerald tried to impose. There was a constant war between the earthy and the precious which often erupted in the afternoons when Gerald was drunk enough to beard the aesthetes in their den.

Melvin filled me in and kept me abreast of all the cross-currents and developments. He was in with the arts boys but also had Gerald's ear, and his Machiavellian disposition kept him alert to every tremor during the day.

The magazine was only a year or so old by the time I joined and had been a huge success, filling a yawning gap in the market gateposted by such old faithfuls as *Playboy* and *Health and Efficiency*. It was Gerald's brainchild; a former Fleet Street court reporter, he had seen a publishing opportunity and backed it with his redundancy money. He subsequently went on to gain widespread notoriety as the dirty old man who lured a young girl out to a desert island to share his Robinson Crusoe fantasy. The two went with a contract from the *Telegraph Magazine* to send back a monthly progress report which Gerald was too lazy to fulfil, and his companion stepped into the breach. Her follow-up book, *Castaway*, turned out to be a bestseller which transferred to the screen with Oliver Reed playing Gerald's role. Every five years since then he popped up in the tabloids trying to pull the same stunt again until he died in 1999.

Quite apart from the theatricals and seedy charm of the office, I also had access again to my beloved Soho. One lunchtime I was tramping back to my duties along Old Compton Street when I drew level with Moroni's newsagents on the other side of the road. At the same moment, an enthusiast in racing gear whipped around the corner from Wardour Street, parked his mount by the kerb and went into the shop. I was rooted to the spot by the sight of his bike; it was almost a Mercier pink which would have been eye-catching enough, but picked out on the downtube in large gold letters was the legend: *PLUME VAINQUEUR*. I could not believe my eyes, they had not rested upon those letters since 1955 at the Grand Prix of Essex. The machine was an amalgam of a whole chapter of my personal cycling history. Its rider then emerged and sat for a moment stowing his paper in a back pocket which gave me time to take him in. He was wearing a horizontally-striped racing jersey of a silky material, and black tights. He was no youngster, in fact his jersey outlined a bit of a paunch, but he looked terrific. I was overwhelmed, although to that part of my mind still stuck in the dress codes of the '50s, he was outrageously attired for a city street. Off-duty riding was conducted by rights in trouser clips and an ex-Korean War combat jacket – but there was no denying his dash and self-possession. Attitudes, confidence, acceptability had obviously evolved to a higher, more flamboyant level – and I wanted to be part of this new more assured cycling. His eventual departure left a vivid impression of riding just for itself; all the old baggage of high hopes and false promises set aside for the simple act of pedalling a good bike in the right clothes. It seemed like a realistic ideal which was well within my grasp. Later that day I decided that the first step would be to give my frame a re-spray and I spent weeks of toil taking the bike down, rigging up a booth and then applying numerous coats from an aerosol spray.

Quicker than expected, I was laid off the Jiffy bags and had to hit the temp trail again. But in '72 my mother died suddenly and I came into possession of the ancestral home, some of which was let so I also inherited a small income.

Shortly after we moved in, the house next door was bought by a young couple with a little boy. They were very friendly and we hit it off immediately. David, the husband, was a keen utilitarian cyclist with a production racer and he responded so well to my tales of club life and racing that we were soon doing a Sunday run together. He was a big, athletic fellow; on a bike he looked like a slightly overweight Francesco Moser.

In '73, Moss, who had prospered in the drug business – parleying his subsidiary Spanish into a management position with a big international company in Madrid – sent me a trade team rig-out for *Casera–Bahamontes* that he had acquired from a mate. What could I do but make my pseudo-professional debut on the Great West Road as a rather blanched Spaniard? It was a liberation and a delight, but going into cafés was a bit of a trial. I couldn't have managed it without big Dave by my side.

In early '74 I persuaded Melvin and one of the arts boys from *Curious*, Michael, to come for a lad's weekend watching the Tour of Flanders. It seemed ridiculously cheap, something like thirty quid all in with Chequers Travel. We boarded the coach at Victoria for a peculiarly subdued departure on the Saturday morning. There was no hint of any rowdiness or high spirits from the predominantly young male assembly. On the contrary, the atmosphere was rather furtive, as if we were setting off on a clandestine mission. Of course, lager louts hadn't been invented then. Only when we were safely underway did a youngster in front of me feel sufficiently at ease to show his colours; he removed his jacket to reveal a tracksuit top with a modest Holdsworth logo on the back.

We passed a pleasant day cruising down to Dover, then eating lunch as we crossed the Channel. Belgium seemed like an endless toytown of little houses with steeply pointed red roofs.

In Ghent we put up at some forgettable pension, but the start the next day was a real treat. At that time there were few barriers and the riders mingled with the crowd. The stars lined up across the road, just a few feet away. There was Gimondi and Moser in the front row, and suddenly Eddy Merckx, arriving at the last minute, weaving through the officials like a great predator.

The weather was typically dull and overcast, but after an hour on the coach the sun broke through. We stopped on the outskirts of a little town where a café was serving Rombout's coffee. There were a few locals out in their Sunday best, but for the most part the town still seemed to be asleep. Suddenly from far off came the insistent crackle of a loudspeaker: *'Pontiac, tick tack. Pontiac, tick tack.'*

Muffled at first, it rapidly became louder and more strident. A specially adapted saloon with a giant, neon-lit metronome on its roof came barrelling through the main street: *'Pontiac, tick tack. Pontiac, tick tack.'*

It was the signal for the inhabitants to come out of their houses and gather at the pavement's edge. A few more publicity vehicles roared through, followed after a while by dawdling outriders on Harley Davidsons. It was all a disconcertingly noisy and fitful overture to the tinkling hush of 200 riders gradually filling the brickwork ravine in the distance and then flooding on towards us like a fine-spun lava flow – all sparkling and multicoloured, serried rank upon serried rank, holding together in perfect unison – their majestic progress took its time to unfold and then rolled itself up again in departure, leaving no trace but a huge sense of awe.

We didn't see much more of the race, certainly not the decisive later stages. Most of the day was spent in traffic jams. Following a race renowned for its many climbs, we never saw a hilltop or even a slope except through the coach window. Everything was sacrificed for a glimpse of the finish, and we only just caught that. Wherever we went on our tailed-back progress, you could see the locals in their cafés, gathered round a TV set catching every move. It struck me then that we would have been better off joining them. In the end, we just made it to the final corner to see Cees Bal, a Dutchman riding for Gan- Mercier, turning into the straight to snatch a lone victory – a result which did not delight the Belgians at all.

Despite all its shortcomings, the trip was judged a great success and became a regular pilgrimage for the next few years.

In 1975, Melvin and I witnessed Eddy Merckx's complete domination in his new rainbow jersey and caught the decisive moment when he dropped his day-long companion, Frans Verbeek, round the back of the finishing circuit – on TV, of course. We were then able to step outside and watch him come home in triumph. We were getting the hang of it. Earlier on, we had even barracked for the inclusion of a vantage-point climb and found ourselves on some obscure difficulty which went up in a series of cobbled ramps. Eddy steamed up it in his brutally efficient fashion with Verbeek clinging on by his eyelashes. Their speed was unbelievable; the turbulence as they roared by rocked you back on your heels. In fact Verbeek's was the ride of the day, a mere mortal managing to stay in the wake of a legend at the height of his powers.

In 1976 we dragged David away from his paternal duties to drive us there in his car. We saw Walter Plankaert triumph after a controversial stand off between Maertens and De Valeminck who were booed on the run-in. This was a daggers-drawn duel which would rumble on through the subsequent Paris–Roubaix (a 'Sunday in Hell' version) to produce the lamentable finale to the following year's Tour of Flanders. David and I were there again to bear witness to something of a swansong rather than a triumph. We were up in a field beside the notorious *Koppenberg* which was buzzing with the news that Merckx was alone in the lead. When he duly turned in upon the hill, he looked imperial in his new Fiat colours – mainly shades of blue, but with the distinctive feature of bright-red overshoes and gloves. Here he was again, going for the exploit and the ground almost shook with the sense of greatness once more thundering its primacy. But unfortunately it all came to nothing; he no longer had the strength of old to carry through such bold initiatives. His early attack foundered like a gambler's last desperate throw. Once caught by Maertens and De Vlaeminck, he packed, leaving his main rivals to settle things between themselves. Roger duly exacted revenge for De Meyer's wheelsucker victory in Roubaix the year before by sitting on the hapless Freddy until, in sight of the line, he jumped away. It was difficult to blame him for applying the same ruthless logic that had been his downfall in the Hell of the North – except for its blatancy. Maertens was riding a silly race anyway, and the rather abject figure that he cut did him no credit at all.

It turned into one of those classics that fall flat instead of gathering to a stirring climax. The underlying truth of the day was perhaps that the race had seen its greatest champion try – and fail – to live up to his finest hours and from then on it went into a spontaneous eclipse.

After an undistinguished season – by his standards – and a desperate search throughout the winter for a new sponsor, the Cannibal found, in early '78, that he no longer had an appetite for riding the bike, much less for the victories that had always made him lick his lips. It was the end of a glorious era.

Somewhere between our Belgian trips during the mid-'70s, Michael introduced me to an up-and-coming young photographer called Brian Griffin. We hit it off immediately because he had been a keen time-triallist as a teenager until hay fever cut short his career. He was using another mutual friend for some experimental portraits and asked me to model for him too. I obliged on several occasions and we became firm friends. Portraiture was his forté and he began to make a reputation for his imaginative shots of leading businessmen for a magazine called *The Director*. This led to a show at the Photographer's Gallery to which I was invited. It promised to be one of those arty occasions when appearances would matter more than usual. I surveyed my sparse wardrobe in despair. After much fruitless deliberation, I dragged out a charcoal tweed three-piece suit – a folly from the '60s that I'd had run up in Burtons for seventeen quid and had hardly ever worn because it was so heavy and chafing on the legs. It was made of a material so thick as to refuse the iron; on the advice of my sales assistant I agreed to have the trouser creases sewn in. I was after the well-to-do country gent look on the cheap, something like J.P. Donleavy on the back cover of *The Ginger Man*. What I got was a three-piece greatcoat that hung on me like chain mail. But in spite of the difficulty I decided to suffer for art and go as a mock pillar of the boardroom. My intuition proved true, the outfit caught Brian's eye and before long I was out cavorting in the park for a singles cover. The art director loved it and we went on to do the album cover for a band called The Rumour – all in the suit. My career as a model was launched.

By the early '80s, I'd been taken up by an agent and was doing background work on commercials as well as photo shoots. My introduction to the big-time took place at Shepperton on the first million dollar commercial directed by Ridley Scott. But my real break came in 1985 when I was chosen to appear in a feature film to be shot in Red China. I had some doubts at first, having suffered a bad case of the gastro-intestinals as a result of a trip to Egypt with Brian earlier in the year. Good sense prevailed however, and one late-October morning I was picked up by a chauffeur-driven white Jaguar which ferried me to Heathrow. There I joined my three companions; we were all to be merchants in a period drama adapted from the book *Tai-Pan*, by James Clavell. We flew to Hong Kong, and then, after an afternoon's rest in a plush hotel, continued on by train across the border to the old tea-trade port of Canton. Night had fallen by the time we arrived and the heat was tropical. Nobody turned up to meet us so we all jammed into a taxi with its windows tight closed and the air-conditioning full on and asked for the White Swan Hotel which was all we knew of the city. Circumstances aboard the cab produced the peculiar sensation of being in a diving bell navigating shoals of dimly outlined cyclists. The streets were lit very haphazardly, if at all, and lights on bikes were obviously considered unnecessary. The majority of the traffic appeared to consist of these shadows moving fluidly on all sides, effectively blotting out any other view. I had arrived in a land where the bicycle was still supposed to be queen of the road – and here, immediately, was the teeming proof.

Later on, I was able to join those shoals; the unit had a bike which was available to anyone who fancied a spin. There were heaps of bikes stacked everywhere, it was like the old days at Herne Hill. Everything was carried by bike too, on amazing contrivances fore and aft. What was impressive was the quietness – except for the bells; the orderliness of it all, and the width of the protected cycle lanes. Nobody seemed to know of any competitive cycling, but I did see a photograph of some racing – the riders were all on the standard sit-up-and-begs that everyone rode. In contrast, when we moved to the old Portuguese colony of Macau, across the bay, little groups of racing-men riding up-to-the-minute lightweights and wearing European trade gear were a regular feature. I saw one sophisticate swoop down the switchbacks to the old harbour sporting a disc wheel – so racing flourished on that side of the water and in Hong Kong too, I should think. But I never found a bike shop.

I returned home in February 1986, laden with presents and still giddy from the high life. My career prospects seemed to have taken an upturn. I felt sure that I could look forward to more such jaunts, but I quickly found that I was back to the old routine of bits and pieces here and there. I met the China crew again at a big commercial shot on the courts of Wimbledon later in the year and we all admitted to a sense of anti-climax.

The Stock Market crash of Black Friday in '87 and the subsequent recession put paid to a lot of advertising and film budgets so the work just dried up. After eighteen months without a call, I was back on my bike again to greet the new decade.

14. Lycra Erotica

During one of my ill-advised and generally disastrous ventures into teaching, I found myself in a girls' school landed with the unruliest of classes for what was called 'French Studies' – my pupils were deemed incapable of the actual language. After covering Paris, the fashion industry and various other girlie topics I scraped the bottom of the barrel for two periods on the Tour de France. My scrapings consisted of odd bits from magazines: posters, maps, a pair of shorts and a jersey. The pièce de résistance was a large, double-page spread from the *Miroir du Cyclisme*: a side view of Georges Talbourdet (the last survivor of the morning break in *A Sunday in Hell*). He is a large, athletic fellow and the shot emphasised the bulky musculature of his legs; they had a Day-Glo sheen that pulsed off the page. I only registered this subsequently because when I put it up there were sighs and stifled squeals.

'Ooh-er, Sir,' said one girl, 'those legs, they make me go all funny.'

I realised then that what I had put before them was a male pin-up; for this class of pubescent teenagers, it was the equivalent of a *Playboy* centrefold.

I covered my confusion as best I could by pressing on, but I was staggered by the realisation that these pictures which I had been devouring for years were actually throbbing with sexuality. Had I simply absorbed the sexual content unknowingly – and enjoyed it? Was all my lifetime's enthusiasm just a cover for secret, unacknowledged longings? Was I a closet gay even to myself? Everything seemed possible in the confusion of those moments as I tried to keep track of the Tour de France.

Later, when I had time to consider, I decided that I wasn't gay, just deluded. In my impressionable youth a giant wedge had been driven between those two grand passions, cycling and sex and I was happy to enjoy both separately – the latter, of course, quite separately. Not even a centre-spread pedalling portrait of a pretty girl with a good figure would have closed that great divide. But where was I likely to see such a thing anyway? The cycling press was overwhelmingly boy's snaps for the boys, and evermore shall be so. The blinkered viewpoint is perpetuated by the forces of inertia and reaction. Around about the same time – the mid '70s – *Cycling*, in a daring break with convention, put the new season's racing gear on a page-three type model instead of the usual sober chap and there was an immediate outcry. The blinds which came down with such a crash then have hardly been tweaked since. And quite right too; why confuse matters, why stir up an already muddied pool? Precisely – in some quarters Eros is still a pestilential little brat, disagreeable, disreputable, disgusting . . . dirty. Much of cycling is lost in a fuddy-duddy world of outdated conservatism. Society at large may have dropped most of its taboos on the subject but the two-wheeled calling seems reluctant to admit its very existence. Is this prurience or outright denial? Neither perhaps; the fascinating possibility presents itself that the lot of us, both male and female, are more at home in the saddle than we are in bed. Maybe we are all party to a peculiar form of wantonness that is obvious to everyone but the participants?

The absence of any profile for gay cyclists (statistically they must be legion) seems to support this view. Where are the gay *coureurs*? When are they coming out of the bike shed? Why is there no pressure to 'out' them, no interest really? Perhaps they fit into the milieu so well, are already and long since so assimilated and comfortably accepted that they feel no need to draw attention to themselves and nor does anyone else. Could it be that the bike unifies all sexual persuasions under the umbrella of its own loftier purposes? What Freud called 'sublimation'?

As I've already indicated, I was brought up on the hard-line, mutual incompatibility of sex and cycling. But there was one event, early in my career, which brought them together in an intimate collusion.

It was late in 1957; I was a well-established member of the club and the swing towards the track had taken place. Cliff Rith (RIP), who had been drafted in for his expertise in that sphere, invited me to a filmshow at Herne Hill track. He had to promise all kinds of delights, including Coppi taking the World Championships in 1953, to win me over because it was a long ride there and back. According to him the whole gang would be going, but on the night they seemed to have discovered previous commitments to wives, girlfriends, TV and good sense, perhaps. Cliff and I had no such ties, so we set out for the South East.

The show took place in the clubhouse and a good crowd had gathered. There was the usual buzz of expectation and after a thorough workout across London I too was ready for some pictorial inspiration. When the lights went down and the projector began to chatter, however, we were greeted with a jerky, coloured sequence of three scantily clad girls giggling at the camera and then running up the side of a hill while losing some of their clothes. This brought hoots of approval from the audience, and, though intrigued, I took it to be just a jokey prelude to the evening's real business. But after a few more such clips my hopes began to be dashed. Exciting though the films were, there was something shameful and embarrassing about sharing them with a group of strangers even in the dark. I ran this kind of thing regularly in my head, but now my guilty little imaginings were being made public on the silver screen. I felt increasingly ill at ease and also indignant. Wasn't it false pretences to drag us all the way over there and then change the programme? This stuff was all very well but what about the *Campionissimo* imposing his iron rule in Lugano? Perhaps they'd move on to cycling in a minute? Faint hopes growing fainter by the minute were my only consolation.

But as scantily clad hussy followed scantily clad hussy, each one more suggestive, I began to entertain graver doubts about the evening's entertainment. My disappointment and unease began to dart away into other misgivings. Wasn't there something very 'off' about using these premises for such shady purposes? They were, after all, the heart of British track sport, host to the Good Friday meet. Did the authorities know? My uneasiness gathered momentum when I realised that our presence was not only sacrilegious but probably . . . *undoubtedly* illegal! We were sitting ducks for a police raid. Even there, tucked away some distance from the road, out of sight and earshot, we were not proof against a tip-off. We would all be carted off to jail. At that very minute helmeted men in dark blue were creeping up on the flickering half-light playing on our curtains. How was I to escape arrest? Making a dash for the exit might only lead straight into the arms of some gloating bobby. Fear and tension broke out across my forehead in a cold sweat, my eyes were wide open in terror, seeing nothing but nightmare projections of apprehension and shame.

A roar from the assembly greeted the appearance of a Gandhi-like figure with a huge member. The innocence of the first sequences had gradually given way to well-scratched black and white footage of twosomes and threesomes committing acts in the flesh which had only been glimpsed in comic strips passed around the classroom and crudely suggested on lavatory walls. It was all horribly true and horribly enthralling. All my panic did nothing to impair the standing ovation from between my legs. Fausto Coppi was obviously a lost cause.

Suddenly, at the end of a particularly squirmy sequence, the lights went up and the projectionist announced that teas would be served through the hatch at the back of the room. The shutter rolled up with a rattle and a final sharp crack. But it was as if the audience had been turned to stone – nobody moved. Hardly anyone even craned round to see what was happening.

We all fought desperately, vainly, to compose ourselves. Eventually someone at the end of the row broke sideways from his chair and bent almost double scuttled to the rear. This eased the deadlock. Various characters on the sidelines who were already standing followed suit, but the main body remained resolutely in place as if still hypnotised by the screen. For my part, I could see no reason to disturb this unanimity; I had decided anyway to forego all refreshment.

When proceedings drew to a close, I was so worked up that I needed immediate release, but instead faced the prospect of a rather uncomfortable hour's ride. My behind hardly touched the saddle; it felt as if I was sitting on the crossbar all the way home.

Once there though, I was able to smuggle my reels of depravity up the stairs to those cool white sheets and, safe in the sleeping household, turn on the projector once again, savouring the moment of choice: where exactly to begin.

There was an unfortunate postscript to our night of delights in South East London. Some time later, while leafing through one of the popular Sundays, I came across a familiar face – it was our projectionist from Herne Hill. He had been caught in the glare of a flashbulb as he unloaded his equipment from a car. 'THIS EVIL MAN,' ran the headline above. The poor bloke had been sent down for running 'blue' filmshows.

There has always been an erotic element in sport. The ancient Greeks, both youths and girls, ran naked in the Pan Hellenic games which celebrated their attractiveness as well as their athletic feats. We are more guarded now, but a certain amount of nakedness has always been necessary for the full freedom of bodily movement and comfort. But a new element of exposure has entered the ring since the introduction of Lycra – especially in cycling. When the old wool shorts gave way to nylon, and then to Lycra in the early '80s, the form beneath the clothing, already an erogenous zone, became more highly charged. Skinsuits, for instance, are just what the name spells out: a second skin, something of a tease to the imagination of onlookers and a blameless opportunity for sexual display to the wearer. Both male and female bodies have been significantly eroticised by this advance in fabric technology. Black cycling shorts have become a fashion classic for women in general because of their comfort and convenience, but primarily for their figure-hugging emphasis. They also have a similar, but less commented-on, impact as a codpiece on the opposite sex. What do racing men wear underneath? – why, nothing but a sewn-in chamois insert for the nether regions. In fact, Lycra shorts perform an outrageous framing of the whole generative area; everything is demurely shrouded, yet at the same time blatantly exposed. Isn't there something flagrantly suggestive about the usual podium pose: the victor's arms spread wide above his head thus throwing his pelvis forward into prominence while vestal virgins either side smile coyly? Is it an accident or by design that his manhood is invariably the centre of the picture? Those shorts convey the subversive touch and shed the stark, black light of Priapus, the god of unbridled fertility. But of course, all this is lost on real enthusiasts, our loins are only charged with a desire to get astride our bikes.

It's a well-known fact that in its heyday snooker on TV attracted a sizeable female audience mainly because of those tensed male cheeks on the edge of the table. How much more stimulating must have been the volume and delineation of Lycra-clad rears in Channel 4's Tour de France coverage. There are no portly old gents in the pro *peloton* either. All the non-cycling women I've met who admitted an enthusiasm for the Tour on telly became rather vague as to the exact focus of interest. Then there were the City Centre crits when the screen would fill to the brim with an orgy of black bottoms *en danseuse*. What a thrill for the ladies; and who knows what inclinations were slipped to the susceptible female consciousness? Maybe a subliminal desire to produce a replica, a well endowed boy-child who would grow to stimulate the same sensations? I have witnessed first-hand my own wife's unrestrained delight in our infant son's *derrière*.

How many keen pedallers and future champions were therefore lost to the sport in the early '90s when a decade of bottom worship was graffitied out of existence? The spoilsport vandals of commerce, ever eager to push up profits, cashed-in the tail-end option for buttock logos. With two squirts of their aerosol cans they both branded the eager steed and neutered their own effectiveness. Now, those well-turned rumps are just another wraparound trademark which all eyes shun. Poor pros – to be subjected to such indignity; when even the cheeks of your arse are hijacked for a sandwich board.

It may take outsiders to spot the characteristic sexiness of cycling which those within are careful to ignore, but sometimes the old tart will lift her hem and show a seamy underside even to the initiate. During my spell as TV critic for *Cycle News*, I switched on for the '97 Ghent–Wevelgem to a close-up of Lars Michaelson's toe cap. From there the camera took a leisurely journey up his leg, dwelling on the striations of his calf, the plump overhang above the knee, the tight outline of his shorts against newly embrocated skin and muscle . . . It pulled back then, over his arm to his chubby, smiling face. He was the compliant Miss Universe contestant offering herself up to the ogling of the multitudes. I've never seen it done quite so obviously since, but this kind of side-show is a feature – certainly of Ghent–Wevelgem – but of other races as well, particularly in Belgium. I was appalled and also intrigued; there was something nauseating about the camera's slavishness until I realised that it was only doing what I would have done had I been on the spot. Now this really was unsettling; the screen had confronted me with my own unconscious voyeurism. What had I been doing in all those years of oblivious eyeballing? Though we use the word loosely, voyeurism is, of course, the technical term for a sexual perversion: watching instead of doing. Was my persistent gawping, both in person and on TV, a perversion? I had a feeling that it probably was.

By its very nature, watching TV is licensed voyeurism, but can it stray beyond the looser sense? For races especially, we see through a glass darkly; the lens pokes its sharp eye in where we literally have no place; it makes us privy to the unguarded intimacy of all-out effort. We are spectral intruders sharply contrasting with the crowds by the roadside who provide a warm human contact, a source of encouragement and support. A furtive gallery, we sit behind a false mirror and devour the action coldly. The riders know better now than to look into the camera, they realise that it is a perilous distraction, they shy away from that vast, blank attention. What they do see of us is but a motorcycle and perhaps a helicopter overhead. As for the camera crew, the driver is watching the road and the cameraman is framing the shot regardless of its content. The whole process is mechanical, detached – in terms of human response, dead.

You may go into raptures when a favourite is doing well, but your hero feels nothing of this. You might experience an almost orgiastic delight should he cross the line first, but it is for yourself alone. How often do you watch a race in company? As soon as you've got the set and the connection, you usually keep a solitary vigil. Just like the riders, you abhor distractions, you've got enough to do without looking out for others. It's really self-pleasuring, isn't it? Could you ever go back to standing by the roadside? Impossible – because your senses now demand the televisual image. Reality is too untrustworthy, too fleeting, much too unsatisfactory; there is no action-replay out there. The only interference you will brook is the commentator, but you can choke him off with the volume control. Then there is just you and the screen, everything focused on and for the eyes, the omnivorous ocular, the pitiless fixity of the voyeur, watching, just watching . . .

In person, the same intensity obtains. There is that thrill of the exemplary body, the trained athlete in the pink of condition, that sense of wonder before such a compendium of exploits, that small shock when familiarity collides with actuality. It's a feeling balanced precariously on the edge of a desire to touch, to assure oneself that this vision is real, to make contact – hence the autograph hunters, the photography, the collection of souvenirs. At this stage there is still a good deal of respect, of distance. But a darker slant can also intrude and the balance can tip towards that cold eye which cuts dead any regard for the person, which scours the star's body as prime bloodstock, as flesh that might be forced to render up its secret. This derives from a more rapacious desire for the same contact, the same possession, but which hatches the doomed plot of inhabiting that body; to taste the exhilaration of such a level of ability and fitness, to appropriate its power. Our eyes can awaken a vampire streak within. The dull spirit of the bystander can be so inflamed with anger and frustration coming face to face with the fulfilled man of action that the mind is short-circuited into potential violence. It is usually only potential; the passive reacting impotently before the active is probably at the core of technical voyeurism. There is a fine line between approbation and appropriation. So beware, watch it; that way stalking beckons.

Despite the overt sexuality of its practices and rituals, cycling has always managed to keep the matter stoutly ring-fenced within its own consciousness up until the last few years. Livelier elements of the specialist press, daringly playing the Page Three card, have tried to help us over the wire by launching an exposé of intercourse before racing – whether to indulge or abstain; top riders reveal their bedroom secrets, etc. Then there was the scientific hoo-ha about inpaired performance and infertitlty. But who gives a chamois insert, anyway? Those prolonged sessions of rumpy-pumpy in the saddle are well worth the risk – aren't they? Wasn't it Sean Kelly who, challenged publicly by his wife as to where she stood in his affections, replied: 'The bike comes first'?

15. Filmshows and Jumbles

'Whatever happened to Chris Brown?' you might ask. After playing such a key role at the beginning he faded rather quickly into the background towards the end of a year and a half of club life. Unfortunately for him in his renegade state, he still lived two doors down from Bo and we would come across him, from time to time, looking rather sheepish. There were no hard feelings, though, on either side; he was such a nice chap that you couldn't hold anything against him. He had become an apprentice electrician and through various 'ton-up kids' in the pool had fallen under the influence of the motorbike. Eventually he graduated to a leather jacket and a Vincent Comet, one of the really 'heavy' bikes of all time. With every credential in place, he hung around the Ace Café on the North Circular almost graduating to Hell's Angeldom. I saw him from time to time in the '60s, but then he bought a house out on Marlow Hill, near where we watched our first race go by. I was unaware of this until I caught up with him again in the early '80s at the end of a roundabout search.

At that time, after two decades of a rather half-hearted literary career, I decided to go commercial and write something about cycling. Martin Ayres took an article for *Cycling* in 1983 and after a good postbag I felt myself launched as a pedal pen-pusher. Beginning work on what was provisionally called 'The Chris Brown Story' which forms the opening chapter of this book, I found myself stumped for the name of his bike – a crucial factor for full authenticity. If necessary I knew I could fake it, but that would take a little conviction out of the blend

– certainly for me. My memory, I felt sure, would eventually come up with the answer, but how long would that take? Finding Chris was out of the question since I hadn't seen him in years. Then one day I spotted him, from the top of a bus, standing outside a local school. There he was, no longer in a leather jacket but sporting a Barbour waxy, the badge of middle-class prosperity. I phoned the headmaster and found that Chris and his wife were pillars of the parents' association. Within a couple of days he rang to announce the surprising news that he now lived just down the road from me. He must have been equally nonplussed by the nature of my reason for seeking him out, but he readily produced the key to the lock of memory: 'Dilecta.'

Since then we have picked up our cycling lives together and he has become the personification of a certain continuity, the embodiment of that spirit which has kept me company throughout my life and lasted so surprisingly into old age. We can re-live that communion which first joined us as boys and perhaps relish its full savour. We can slip away on Saturday afternoons for a potter around Richmond Park; it's a promenade, a mobile chat, really. For us the bike performs one of its most winning attributes: a means of escape. It sets us free of the family, the household, the responsibilities of a paterfamilias. When we can, we try to get away, but what do we talk about? – the family, the household, the responsibilities of a father figure. Gradually though, the bike works its sorcery, and turning the pedals restores us to that essential, boundless freedom.

Around the park we sometimes come across the zealot vet, David Stanton. He is there every day, winter and summer, and he captains an early morning clubrun on Sundays from Richmond Gate which gets him back indoors for lunchtime after doing 70 miles minimum. Not that his activities are confined just to the park – anything but. He has a house near Toulon and regularly ferries groups over to France to take part in *cyclo sportives*. An exemplary figure in all departments, he attains a real aristocratic level of indulgence in the manner of his telly watching; he has installed a French TV plus all the equipment so that he can enjoy the fuller and deeper coverage from across the Channel. For the last few years I have nourished the hope that one day, after a season of regular outings and a fortnight's intensive training on holiday in Somerset, I might join him on one of his Sunday runs and see how far I could get. Chris, perhaps wisely, has never really committed himself to this scheme and now, after my wife insisted last year on holiday that I accompany her on a walk rather than cycling in the afternoons, I have this image of David – at 67 already a half decade ahead of us – gradually pulling away in the distance, never to be caught.

In the early years of our resumption of activities, we enjoyed the added diversion of taking Chris's son Matthew out to races. He was in the Archer and one Sunday we took him out to the Green Street Green circuit. There on the hill, officiating as prime judge, was Chas Messenger, my old club captain and national leading light since the war. What loyalty, what longevity, what devotion to the sport. But he was only one among many; the faces we knew in our youth still seemed to be running things. It was heart-warming but also a little sad; one had the feeling that this side of the sport might be on its last legs. Derek Worsley was still running the Grand Prix of Essex until last year and Stuart Benstead continues with the Archer; no doubt there are countless examples from the rest of the country. The omnipresence of vets runs right through every department of the sport; it is, I suspect, an international phenomenon.

A quiet but fundamental change has taken place on the back of shorter working hours, increased remuneration and earlier retirement – but above all through different attitudes. In the '50s you were an old man at 30. The curtain came down on youthful frivolity and you prepared for the long slog of setting up home and starting a family. 'Settling down', it was called, which would take you through to the slippers and cardigan of retirement. It was a grim prospect, but generally accepted; a man had to do what a man had to do. But as the '60s gained momentum all these received notions came under fire. Mature self-sacrifice could no longer hold out under the barrage of heedless self-indulgence. It was all easy, man; you danced till you dropped, and maybe if you danced hard enough, you wouldn't even drop. The elixir of eternal life was in the air and all ages took hefty lungfuls. A new agenda was set, outlooks were revised; every generation since has pursued headlong consumption while steadfastly refusing to be consumed. They just continue doing what they've always done, and those ahead of them, released by early retirement, redundancy, whatever, have grabbed the opportunity to return to cycling full-time and smash the times that they achieved in their youth.

One of the most remarkable examples of this phenomenon is Brian Haskell who won the vet's Best All-Rounder in 1999 at the age of 70 with times of 56 minutes, 16 seconds for 25 miles; 1 hour, 51 minutes, 28 seconds for 50 miles, 4 hours, 19 minutes, 20 seconds for 100 miles and 12 hours for approximately 248 miles – his 50-mile time a staggering 9½ minutes better than what he managed aged 25 in 1954. This achievement was celebrated by a feature in *Cycling Weekly* by Keith Bingham which showed a black and white shot of him coming third in the BLRC (British League of Racing Cyclists) Independent Championship of 1957. There he is, crossing the line, already looking an old man with his thinning hair. By that time, of course, he was getting on – 28, coming up to hanging his wheels. But – sign of things to come – he persisted for another six years, until he was way over the hill at 34. More or less the age he might pass for on his monocoque carbon frame with rear disc wheel, his head conveniently hidden beneath an aero helmet (see picture 14). But nine-and-a-half minutes – surely none of this can explain such a yawning gap against the grain of age? The size of his chainwheel might hold a clue. Perhaps this is the crucial difference: everyone was stuck in little gears back then. Why, 73-inch fixed was a respectable ratio for a 25 in 1954 – remember the twiddling Higginson twins? Very few even considered gears. Brian is probably heaving round something nearly twice that these days.

Incidentally, there is a gallery of teenagers just by the finishing line in the black and white shot who are dressed in the all-purpose cycling rig-out of that era: an ordinary collar and tie shirt open at the neck, a long-sleeved woollen jersey, jeans with trouser clips and soft, flat-soled cycling shoes – the same outfit, with a change of shoes, that would stand you in good stead down at the youth club. It wasn't only the gears that were restricted in those days. In fact, comparison of the two pictures reveals a monumental leap in quality of life and expectations. If the same trend continues, we could foresee a centenarian turning in times on a par with our Brian in the same span projected into the future, say 2045. On current form he might be there to witness it.

Chris and I are unlikely to be standing beside him. We are some distance from competition let alone improvement; our sights are set steadily on the past.

Because we are still equipment fetishists at heart, another prized sortie is to cycling jumble sales. We go out early of a Saturday morning to join the queue at Giggs Hill Green Community Centre – next to where the Milk Race used to start – in early January for the first event of the new year. They are curious affairs, these one-day sales, almost entirely a vet's preserve, both buyers and sellers being of a certain age. The whole promotion has the effect of reversing one's youthful experience of bike shops. At jumbles the customers are in the majority; we descend mob-handed on these makeshift malls and the sales assistants are welcoming and eager to please. They have laid out the fruits of their labours, they want you to fondle and admire as much as to buy. It's all their own work, they are artists of the found object and its arrangement in the same way as a more conventional practitioner might hang his pictures in a gallery. They are well disposed to confer with a knowledgeable and appreciative public – qualities which have

149

difficulty in surviving the first ten minutes. For our part, once the doors are opened and we get a whiff of that intoxicating bouquet of grease, oil, old leather and rubber, sweaty knitwear and yellowing paper plus the redolent undertones of various metals, our nostrils flare and we are seized by a bargain hunter's frenzy. The stallholders must look on in dismay as this jostling horde mills around with downcast gaze, poking and rummaging, weighing and measuring until something else catches their eye and they dart off.

After that first mad hour, the furore settles; the bargains have been snapped up and tea taken, perhaps with a slice of home-made cake. Old friends are greeted and chance acquaintanceships struck up; intention has loosed its grip and in that relaxation the senses are more alert. It is then that the real work of the morning may commence, the more measured second circuit when we can allow ourselves to browse at leisure; we are looking for something but we don't know what. We are still under the impression that the search is for some vital accessory, but what really draws us back is the call of memory. These jumbles are also archivists' conventions; a whole seam of history is collected together piecemeal in the form of artefacts, a vast memory bank is laid out to tease individual recall.

The real thrill of the morning is when your eye falls upon some obscure glint of recognition, some shine, even some blank opacity which leads awareness towards one of those dark vaults of forgetfulness that then opens in a flash and a fragment of your past is delivered up whole and vivid. Beneath the roof of the community centre we all become Proustians in search of lost time, and those shoe-boxes of pitted chrome and dulled alloy, those moth-eaten jerseys and faded start-sheets are our *madeleines*.

Then of course, there is the sideshow of characters: the old boy with the handlebar moustache who is a dead ringer for Maurice Garin, the first Tour winner; the chap in a Norfolk jacket and knickerbockers who might have just alighted from an Old Ordinary; the Frank Patterson look-alike in baggy plus-fours smoking a straight-stemmed pipe and the senior citizens in washed-out trade gear from the Hinault era, bent by years of crouching on the drops, whose faces beneath their pixie caps have been lined by countless headwinds – they form a huddle like garden gnomes in a lawnmower commercial. Here and there some pukka racing man hobbles by in his clog-soled silver dreamboats. Everywhere the near-decrepit jostle with the suavest of smart casuals, evidence that the bike appeals to all manner and conditions of men. And women. They are there too, but mainly in a subsidiary role, as back-up to their husbands and minders for the kids – whole families have turned out. But this is predominantly a bloke's affair, although overall it presents a vision like one of those old masters depicting a teeming medieval fair. The ruck, the turmoil, the things you missed and should have bought, the impulse buys that you now regret, the whole head-swimming whirl – when it all becomes too much you totter doorwards to emerge dazed and confused into the grey midday.

And there, parked against an outside wall is an old, resprayed H.E. Green with original transfers giving the address in Dawes Road. Chris takes down the number with a view to seeing what has replaced that ancient landmark cycle shop – his office is nearby. Further examination reveals brazed-on cantilever brakes – surely a rarity when it was built – with an unbored fork crown to confirm the intent. What is that down by the front drop-out? An even more whimsical touch – a tiny, belt driven cyclometer! Our cup runneth over. Eventually we reel away to the car, giddy with a kind of drunkenness.

The jumble leads on to my own small promotion – what else but a filmshow? I work the queue beforehand to distribute flyers and once inside flypost where I can. It is the last chance to reach the target audience because the show usually takes place on the next weekend. With Christmas quickly gone, bad weather and the first races hardly on the horizon, late January can seem like the endless night of the cycling year. What I wanted to do was shine a little light in the darkness. I've always enjoyed those low-key close-season festivals, that coming together of a long winter evening to enjoy the reflected glow of high summer. Filmshows usually provide that sense of well-being and conviviality which comes of gathering round a generously banked fire when it's cold outside.

In the early '90s I was introduced to Ed Lewis, the cinema director of Riverside Studios, the local arts complex. He runs one of the best repertory houses in London, rivalling the National Film Theatre for range and depth. He is also a commuting cyclist, and this plus the fact that he lives nearby brought us together. I would come across him on his way home from work and badger him into showing old Antonionis and Godards until it dawned on me that his cosy little auditorium with its proximity to a bar and café would make an ideal venue for a cycling show. He bought the idea immediately so I contacted Mr Filmshow himself, Ray Pascoe, and we set about putting a programme together.

We were over-ambitious at first, we did two shows in the launch year, 1997, clearing out gems like *A Sunday in Hell* and *La Course En Tête*, the Eddy Merckx story. So for '98 we were looking for other ways to bulk out the afternoon's fare.

It struck us that several items on the supporting bill – home-based classics of the '60s and '70s – often featured riders who were still active in one way or another. We decided to contact them and see if they would come along to introduce a live element into the proceedings. The inaugural London–Holyhead of 1962 seemed a likely runner. Ray got a verbal promise from Dennis Tarr, the winner, but that was the last we were to hear of him. I had more luck with the third-placed rider, Doug Collins, who has long been the moving spirit behind the Twickenham CC, one of the most successful London clubs. He and Tarr were teammates for what turned out to be a Condor–Mackeson benefit, getting two on the podium and the team prize. On the afternoon of the show I was still hoping that Tarr would turn up, but that hope proved to be in vain. Albert Roberts, though, did; he was another Condor rider who had come along out of interest and he proved to be a godsend. Doug and he went into a hilariously dry double act which closed the show on an unprecedented high note. Since then the live finale has become the highlight of the show; we have entertained and been entertained by Tony Gowland, Geoff Wiles and Phil Corley. The key seems to be that the star guests enjoy themselves as much as the audience; the bond which joins us all is made into a living reality.

One of the subtle intimations of advancing years is that glance which strays towards the obituaries. The broadsheet dailies, led by *The Independent*, started the trend and *Cycling Weekly* has followed suit. We are all getting older together and as we totter forward we want to know who has fallen – it's the '60s generation again. In cycling terms these notices are increasingly a sombre measure of the danger on the roads. Week by week they record the toll of death there which is disquieting enough, but over the last few years they have contained a specially poignant inlay: the sudden demise of men and women who have been devoted bike riders all their lives and have found distinction thereupon only to be savagely cut down while in the saddle. I'm thinking of course of Pete Longbottom, Edie Atkins, Ken Warren and even Loic le Floic – a little known French pro from the '80s whose name in its play of vowels and consonants seemed to summon up the essence of pedalling. He was killed in 1998 on his way to a clubrun.

These notices invariably contain that grisly euphemism: 'in collision with a motor vehicle.' It is, I suppose, some *sub judice* constraint applied by the courts, but how ghoulish it sounds in its attempt to draw a veil over what was undoubtedly an act of blood-spattered carnage. How galling, too, the inference of mitigation towards some heedless motorist who 'just didn't see' the victim. The notoriously callous pro-driver stance of the judiciary in these matters – and of course the general motoring public – has been highlighted recently through the casual slaying of Bruce Bursford, an innovative bike builder and record breaker, who was cut down by a lorry driver distracted by his mobile phone. The culprit was prosecuted not for manslaughter, but for driving without due care and attention, getting off with a five-hundred-pounds fine and a one-year ban. Motorists everywhere are driving without due care and attention in what cannot be anything else but a conscious effort to make the roads safe only for themselves.

Wild hybrids of man and machine command the highways. Driven by infernal combustion, huge mechanical pachyderms and their smaller offspring stampede wherever the way is tarred and levelled. We can only keep out of their way and try not to enrage them further. In fact, they mean us no harm for the most part; the poor things are in the grip of some contemporary St Vitus' dance. Many of us know what it is like to be part of that crazed herd, you lose your head, you become a blunt instrument, you enter humanity's death throes.

But the motor vehicle is also a vet, it has had its century. The seeds of its own extinction have always been pulsing away beneath those bonnets. Like a powerful drug its graph of influence soars to a jagged peak and then plummets into self destruction. Eventually the mad monsters will run out of road and they know it, they know it now in their tailbacks and traffic jams – it is the fuel of their frustration and their rage. That stretch of open road where you can put your foot down and feel the original high is well into diminishing returns. The opium of the people has been cut and cut by its own proliferation and the withdrawal symptoms are merciless.

There will come a day of terminal gridlock when everyone will be obliged to slam the driver's door and walk away from motoring – for ever. When the wreckage is cleared the meek shall inherit the motorway, time-triallists will come into their rightful dragstrips, spaghetti junction criteriums will become the new rage. Or maybe the leftovers won't be cleared, perhaps those acres of tarmac will be gradually filled by the detritus of an era of misused resources; those flyovers and embankments become a huge breaker's yard, a national monument to a disastrous love affair.

What will become of all those four-wheeled implements of violence and oppression? Inevitably they will be recycled into two-wheeled conveyances of peace and liberation.

Okay, it's a dream, but even the superannuated can dream. The truth is that whatever the threat posed by traffic, whatever the danger, we still respond to the call of the road, that path which has served us so well, so bounteously. As the years accumulate, the reading of magazines, the telly-watching, even the chat, give way more and more to what one really cherishes: the act of riding a bike.

In the spring of 1998, *L'Equipe* ran a feature on Eddy Merckx inaugurating a cycle route dedicated to his name. There he was in the accompanying picture, a porkier version, stretching his winter gear on the approach to the Kwarement, surrounded by his former *domestiques*, men who saw out their careers doing donkey work for him: Victor Van Schil, Jos Huysmans, Deschoenmaecker. Gloved and helmeted though mudguardless despite the road's wetness – this was the day after the Tour of Flanders – they were hitting the climb at the front of the bunch just as in the good old days. What emerged from the article was the fact that they had lost little of that professional discipline which had dominated their former life. 'I ride all the time,' said Van Schil, 'it keeps you healthy.' At 58 he had already put 5,000 kilometres into his legs that year. '*Rouler, toujours rouler, c'est bon pour la santé*,' might well be the rallying cry of all vets. It is certainly the theme of that marvellous little video, *Vas-y, Lapebie*, an idiomatic translation of which could include that old gallery chant of encouragement: 'Up, up, Lapebie.' Roger, a Tour winner in 1937 and a laureate of Paris–Roubaix, as well as being, at 80, a glowing endorsement of the benefits of lifelong cycling, is seen in the concluding sequence riding to a deserted beach and leaning on his faithful machine before a sunlit seascape, where he makes a frank and heartfelt admission: 'I tell you this, I love my bike more than myself.' At the water's edge of his own approaching mortality, as it were, he seems to recognise that the bike is greater than one human life, that it somehow represents the eternal.

16. Writing the Bike

One great bonus for the urban enthusiast is the ready access to *L'Equipe*, the French sporting daily. On the Monday after Andrei Tchmil's superb victory in the Millennial Tour of Flanders, I was able to savour a large coloured picture of him forcing the pace on the Bosberg which dominated the front page (broadsheet) and inside, two full pages of report and comment. Now that's a treat, a real lunchtime feast.

In the early '90s, *L'Equipe* began to be available here on the day of issue, previously you had to wait till the Tuesday. But whatever the day, it has always provided the most informed, comprehensive and most passionately involved of coverages. I can't say I understand every word, and I undoubtedly miss a lot of the references and wordplay, but even then it is still the most satisfying journalism in any language.

Here is the Tchmil report in my own translation:

> THE TRIUMPH OF AN OLD HAND
> Yesterday afternoon, Belgian fans, whose national pride makes them reluctant to see the *Ronde* fall to anyone but their own, didn't know whether to rejoice at the success of Andrei Tchmil – leader of the Lotto team and their adopted countryman, though his past reputation inclines to controversy – or to relapse into the same disillusion which had reduced them to a stunned silence on the hushed announcement that Johan Museeuw's bold lone break at the foot of the Mur de Grammont had been swallowed up by the chasers.

157

'King' Johan had taken the bull by the horns in jumping away on the first slopes of the celebrated Mur. There were fifteen kilometres to go, including the climb of the Bosberg. Clinging to the hillside, beers in hand, flags waving, the Flemish hordes joined together in a guttural chant of *'Ole! Ole! Ole!'*, a kind of hymn to the glory of their champion who seemed to have made the decisive move. One sprint was all it took to launch him a good thirty metres in front of the rucking *peloton* which was embroiled in partisan quarrels, while in its midst, Peter Van Petegem, his immediate national rival, was just beginning to feel the effects of a prolonged expenditure of energy.

On the bulging cobbles which rise up to the holy chapel of Grammont, the Belgian crowd were ready to believe that this version of the *Ronde* was about to add itself to that ceaselessly enriched scroll of honour already attached to their hero's name – that Museeuw, who had already triumphed three times in these parts, would emerge victorious yet again and thus become the event's outright record-holder.

But appearances were deceptive. A shadow seemed to hang over this sovereign vision of a Museeuw up in arms, throwing himself body and soul into the struggle as is his wont, for there appeared to be some hint of laboriousness, the sense of a rider diminished by the after-effects of his crash two years before in the Arenberg forest, an accident whose real impact and consequences to his career we will possibly never fathom.

The Flemish supporters had reached the highest pitch of exaltation, the echo of their cheers was still ringing around the countryside when Museeuw seemed to mark time and then be caught after a spectacular chase by Stefan Weisemann, Eric Zabel's henchman, and then less hurriedly by those such as Tchmil, Van Petegem and Vainsteins. At this point the action went off the boil, oracular predictions died away, and the *Ronde* seemed to founder in that stalemate which certain observers had already deplored a fortnight previously at the finish of Milan–San Remo.

That made for more than six hours of racing since the bunch left Bruges, and what had we seen during those 250 kilometres plus, but the lowly Eric de Clercq pursuing a morning break beyond the bounds of ordinary good sense – a move which was as pointless as it was courageous. Subsequently Wauters, Serpellini and Tafi pedalled forward to rock the bandwagon, whipped on by the stalwarts of Farm Frites: Klier, Ivanov and Van Petegem, who were much in evidence once the climbs began, but although the trio's daring initiative showed great merit, it was also, in the end, to little avail.

The Revenge of a Judas

A certain paralysis seemed to have overtaken the favourites; a bunch numbering as many as 30 riders came together at the bottom of the Bosberg which is only twelve kilometres from Meerbeke. One began to fear for a bunch sprint, that symptom of rather sterile racing, lacking in imagination and endeavour, which we have come to see too much of, and which plays straight into the hands of the sit-in merchants who, of course, have become more and more numerous.

But it was then that Andrei Tchmil pulled off the impossible by slipping away on the descent from the Bosberg. A Tchmil who has always proved so adroit at retrieving a difficult situation. A Tchmil more enterprising than usual, who had first shown himself on the Berendries climb where he replied in person to an attack by Lampre's resident Pole, the workmanlike Zbigniew Spruch. A Tchmil – well backed up by Thierry Marichal – who had sensed more than anyone else the urgency of some counter behind Tafi when the latter took off to join Serpellini and Wauters on the Korteleer. A Tchmil, moreover, who had never budged from Van Petegem's wheel on all the strategic climbs, to the point where the Flandrian was completely rattled by such obsessive marking. A Tchmil, finally, who threw off this more accustomed role on the Mur de Grammont to chase Johan Museeuw before delivering the knockout punch, conscious, as he was, that he had everything to fear from a big bunch finish against the likes of Vainsteins and Zabel who were already frisking with impatience at the head of affairs.

Alone in the lead, the Lotto captain succeeded in gaining ten seconds, then twenty – a substantial gap which was to decline appreciably. He had no more than fourteen seconds with four kilometres to go, only ten at the three kilometre banner; to the point where there was general apprehension – particularly with the late rush of a resurgent Ekimov as well as Weisemann working for Zabel – that the *peloton* would manage to bring him back. Happily though, Andrei Tchmil succeeded in keeping enough in hand to carry off the classic of his dreams.

This represents just half of the main report. There was also a move-by-move summary, the complete finishing list, comments by the principal also-rans, a section on the performance of the French and a complete update on the World Cup rankings. On the opposite page there was a feature interview with Tchmil and reports on various lesser French events plus a note on Ullrich's latest forfeiture. As is usual, the next day's edition saluted the weekend's big winner with almost a whole page devoted to a potted biography and a verbatim account of his classic wins under the headline: TCHMIL, A MONUMENT.

Such an amount of space and attention is no less than a

French victor would have had showered upon him. *L'Equipe* consistently rises above any nationalistic bias; it celebrates the sport for itself pure and simple. For instance, when Graham Obree broke the hour record in '93, as a comparative unknown, he was given the whole front page. It is this open-heartedness as well as the expertise of its writers that gives its opinions and judgements so much weight. But the key to its day-to-day appeal resides in that characteristic tone of voice, that special language which rolls across the page and down the columns, that layering of clause upon clause, those sentences which circle and circle to pin down a special atmosphere, the painstaking evocation of the day and its deeds. Prose narrative of this order has the ability to stop and expand the moment, to scour its depths and significance, to dig out its secrets. At its best it demonstrates the almost infinite flexibility of the written word and rises to the epic pitch of the events which it describes. Far from being displaced by live TV, *L'Equipe* proves a necessary complement because it provides a vivid recapitulation in another medium. Electronic actuality is so hurried, so driven by the need to keep up with the action that we often require a slow motion re-run to fully explain what we have seen. The two perspectives round out and deepen the experience, but the newspaper you can take out to lunch.

L'Equipe can play the oracle, the stern lobbyist and the giddy enthusiast with equal grace because it is shot through with that reasoned and heartfelt passion we all share. In its pages one can keep up with the living history of the sport as it unfolds day by day. More than that, by simply picking it up we are in touch with one of the flimsy but durable foundations of the sport itself. We all know that the Tour de France was the brainchild of Henri Desgrange, the editor of *L'Auto* which subsequently became the paper whose praises I am singing here. *L'Equipe* is itself a monument.

The pen and the pedal have always been intimately coupled because, in the beginning, races could be seen by vast crowds, but only in fleeting glimpses. Newspapers provided the only answer to those questions which were on every watcher's mind: what happened? And who won? So big circulations were built on this free show and proprietors began organising the events which poured money into their coffers. That spontaneous love-match has now become a well-seasoned marriage.

Another factor which brought wheel and word to the altar was the fascination of artists. At the turn of the nineteenth century, cycling was a fashion fad available to all but the lowest levels of society. It captured the imagination of the most imaginative: painters painted it, poets rhymed it and novelists set their characters pedalling. Tolstoy, for instance, learned to ride a bicycle at the age of sixty-seven in 1895. He went further; on a subsequent trip to Paris he discovered competitive cycling and returned with a subscription to *La France Cycliste* in his pocket. Once back home, it came to light that track racing took place at Tula, south of Moscow, and he paid the place several visits.

The European intelligentsia were enthralled and have continued to be so to this day. The French especially have maintained a proprietorial respect for and passionate interest in the sport for which they invented such distinctive forms and this concern translates into high standards for its general dissemination. Well-known authors regularly vie for the chance to follow a stage of the Tour and their books celebrate the sport's established position in the cultural heritage.

No such history or standards obtain on this side of the Channel, unfortunately. In 1894, the year before the first Paris–Roubaix was run, F.T. Bidlake, our resident Quisling, was selling out the sport to the motoring lobby by inventing the shifty cult of time-trialling. The golden moment which called for enterprise and imagination was brushed aside and fell into an unmarked grave. Decades passed in weekly Remembrance Sundays as black-clad figures gathered at dawn on deserted country roads to expiate this grovelling act of appeasement. Racing went into mourning for itself and remained in widow's weeds until the Second World War. Ironically, these services still persist today, but are now conducted in the more self-confident apparel of the continental tradition that we might well have emulated but for our lily-livered officials.

Great strides have been made since Brian Robinson embarked on his pilgrimage to the Promised Land in 1955, but he, and other prophets who have arisen to follow his example have since found little honour in their own country because of the grim rancour of Bidlake's heirs.

We had turned tail and run before we were born and were delivered into defeatism and myopia – that was our tradition and we are still trying to shake off its dark shadow. Small wonder then that no one from the larger culture has seen fit to notice us let alone find anything worth recording until Channel 4 started transmitting the Tour.

But there are signs that all this is about to change. One of the acknowledged mandarins of English letters, Julian Barnes, as recently as 1995, turned his pen to the depiction of cycle racing in his short story 'Brambilla'. It first appeared in the Christmas issue of *The Spectator*, which was something of a surprise, but the historic weekly continues to be quite cycle-friendly.

Brambilla is, of course, the unfortunate who lost the 1947 Tour to Robic on the last day, but Barnes resurrects a lesser-known facet of his character to make him an exemplar of the indomitable courage of the professional racing man.

As far as I know, the author has little experience of cycle racing except for a wide reading about it in both French and English, but he shows a sure understanding of the mythology which underpins the sport: how every significant pedal turn is back-lit by the luminaries of the past and how this play of light, both far and near, is the process by which the tradition maintains and renews itself. Thus his tale is based upon the three necessary perspectives: present practice and aspiration, the past of living memory and the legends who line the horizon like a ring of guiding stars.

In the story, Andy and his girlfriend Christine have taken off to France, he to become a pro racer and she to get away from a stifling home background. Andy introduces himself by describing how Mr Douglas, his hometown mentor, had taught him the finer points of descending and as a final lesson had passed on the legend of Brambilla. (As readers we have to wait for the concluding paragraph to discover the great man's full significance, but the story's title is neatly justified.)

Christine then takes up the narrative by filling in the details of their flight into exile plus Andy's reverence for Sean Kelly (the second perspective). The Irishman then becomes the focus of both narratives as Andy fights to complete his first Tour and Christine struggles to understand his motivation while herself adapting to the gruelling routine of a *Folies Bergère*-type floorshow. They both bring their talents to typically French institutions and forge their characters therein. It is the story of a twofold initiation.

I hope the foregoing has whetted your appetite for the bracing range and ingenuity of this work because I don't want to spoil the pleasure of reading it. There is, however, one small detail that I would like to pick up on. In the first section, Andy says: 'like a jump or whatever'. Now this short phrase won me over immediately to the authenticity of Andy's voice. I've noticed since that Barnes has an uncanny ability (i.e. the fruit of hard and clear-sighted labour) to enter the lives of his characters by displaying a pitch-perfect command of their vernacular. This seemingly inconsequential line, so throwaway, is a good example of his mastery. We can only hope that he pursues his researches into our wheeler's world and comes up with another comparable feat. Just recently, he did just that by writing a survey of drug-taking in cycle racing ('TERMS OF ENDURANCE', *The Guardian*, Saturday Review 26 August 2000) which was so thoroughly researched, so well balanced and authoritative, and generally eloquent as to usher him straight into the front rank of cycling commentators. You will find 'Brambilla' in his collection *Cross Channel*, published by Jonathan Cape.

Hot on the heels of Julian Barnes's story came Blake Morrison in 1996. Morrison started out as a poet and editor and latterly made his name with a distinctive memoir entitled *And When Did You Last See Your Father?* In between times he kicked off a lively series of talks for Radio 4 called 'Better than Sex' with a celebration of the joys of cycling in rural Suffolk. This was quickly snapped up by *The Guardian* for its G2 supplement. Morrison here describes the delights of recreational pedalling in the country. He distances himself from any of the more partisan forms of cycling like racing and urban commuting, he only rides near his holiday home close to the sea, but the simple pleasure he finds there is compellingly rendered. His enthusiasm is based upon long years of forced abstinence which became a guilty secret – he didn't learn to ride until his late twenties. So he brings all the fervour of a late conversion to his discovery. There are some pointed comments about the kinship of sex and cycling but he only toys with the implications of the series' title before brushing these aside. The strength of the piece lies in its sincerity and wit, and the fluent grace with which it is told. You can find it in his recent collected journalism, *Too True*, published by Granta. The piece is called 'Two Wheels Good'.

Another young turk with a pronounced interest in cycling is the novelist Philip Hensher. He came out as an enthusiastic pedaller in his review of the reprint of Paul Kimmage's *Rough Ride* published in the *Spectator* just before the infamous '98 Tour. When the scandal broke he wrote very perceptively about the drug problem in his column in the *Independent*. The London Cycling Campaign also collared him for their 'My bike and I' feature. I think we can count him as a true fan.

Michael Ignatieff, a commanding interviewer, presenter of TV arts programmes and latterly a novelist and writer has also enthused in print about watching the Tour go by.

Graham Robb, the recent biographer of the French poet Arthur Rimbaud, added himself to the numbers too with a gracefully informed and sharply knowing review of Lance

Armstrong's *It's Not About The Bike* and another of an anthology of cycling literature by Edward Nye in the *Times Literary Supplement*.

We can only hope that these relative youngsters will follow the lead of that elder statesman, Julian Barnes, and significantly enlarge the literature of cycling.

On the specialist front, there are two searching studies of the modern-day Tour by Geoffrey Nicholson and Robin McGowan. But the big event of the last decade was the publication and timely reprint of Paul Kimmage's *Rough Ride*. I remember coming across the original dispatches in a Christmas issue of *Cycling* and being spellbound. Here was the story of 95 per cent of the *peloton*, the also-rans, the *domestiques*, the poor devils fighting to stay in the race, which said much more about the heroism and dedication of the profession than another million star profiles. It was heart-rendingly poignant; the silent majority had found a voice and for ever after they would be there, more eloquently mute, crowding the edges of all the big occasions. Those figures making for the dressing rooms or the hotel, those downcast pedallers just beating the time limit, the injured and the defeated – you could no longer turn a blind eye; they were part of the action as well, and theirs was perhaps the greater drama.

Freddy Maertens' biography (*Fall From Grace*) had the same effect; the chaos and contradictions of his personality springing from the page to confirm the chaos and contradictions of his career.

Graham Watson has proved himself almost as good a writer as he is a photographer. *The Road to Hell* makes a telling case for the one-day classics as being at the heart of cycle racing. They have managed to retain their authenticity and a scale which allows them to fit comfortably into the new extended season – in fact, to thrive. Graham lovingly describes their individual traits and idiosyncrasies from his privileged vantage point. There is a wonderful passage early on when he recounts the birth of his vocation as a cycling photographer.

In his youth he rode across northern France to come upon Francesco Moser in full flight over the cobbles on his way to victory in Paris–Roubaix. It proved to be a moment of revelation which changed his life. Here he pinpoints the heart-stirring appeal of these one-day races and the prowess which they bring forth, that marvellous showcasing of style and class, the sense of the sublime which his pictures often convey.

Chris Sidwell's recent *Mr Tom* is a passionately delivered redemption of his uncle's name which sets new standards of intelligence and documentation in cycling biography – an enthralling read.

Of course what we all read most of is the ordinary bread-and-butter reporting in newspapers and the cycling press. David Walsh, who writes for *The Times* is, to my mind, the most stylish and perceptive of commentators. He has a deep knowledge and appreciation of the sport which he wears lightly. Tim Hilton, who used to write for *The Guardian* and is now with *The Independent*, is another whose work is worth seeking out. He did a brilliant introduction to the Tour in 1987 which is still a benchmark.

As to the cycling press, I find it irritatingly laced with slipshod Americanisms. Back in 1985, a new glossy monthly called *Winning* appeared on the shelves when there was a dearth of such material available. I liked the pictures and the general presentation but I rarely shelled out because it was written in a mangled stateside English which had all the taste and substance of the equally spurious hamburger. Since then that pre-digested gobbledegook has become the staple of cycling journalism, thus lowering standards of reporting and commentary generally. Riders are no longer 'in,' they are 'at' a race – blurring the difference between being in the bunch and standing at the roadside. Despite a Tour being self-evidently a process rather than a place, we get absurdities like 'at the Giro'. There was a time when all other prepositions seemed to have been wiped from the dictionary, when every hack appeared to be going for the World 'At' Record. Then there are those vague umbrella phrases like 'off the pace' or 'riding tempo' which are used for a multitude of situations described far more vividly by real English terms like: 'dropped', 'tailed off' and 'shot out the back', or in the second case here: 'chasing hard', or 'eyeballs out'. One of my favourite yankeeisms is 'drafting'. Who is drafting whom you might ask, and what does this draft consist of? It sounds like one of their prissy euphemisms – for farting, perhaps? Who but the tone-deaf would drop this clanger when the far more evocative 'slipstreaming' is to hand, or the picturesque 'sitting on a wheel', to say nothing of 'fanning out in an echelon'. Our media mouthpieces are pushing aside a whole more colourful vocabulary for these nauseating fast-food options. Americanisms blur and deaden the native precision and vividness of our mother tongue. I sympathise with poor journos having to churn out the same old fodder week after week, but I also have some respect for my stomach – those chemically enhanced nuggets refuse to go down. Alasdair Fotheringham is almost alone in penning a wholesome line, for keeping abreast of the news these days is often on a par with a rake through the litter bin outside McDonalds.

Like the Gadarene swine we are being possessed by this transatlantic swill, and eventually we will drown in it. Who really wants to become the fifty-first state? In that so-called 'Land of the Free' there are forty-one million who can't even afford to go to the doctor. Every time we pick up one of their dud coinages the deeper we wade into their crazed sea.

The whole thing is bigger than cycling, of course, but the sport has been quicker than most to vulgarise itself and be lured away from its essentially European roots. Coca-Cola, along with a host of other dollar brand names, has colonised the Tour and now Lance Armstrong, from beneath his burger cap, is refusing to speak French. Though usually veiled in a folksy affability, we should recognise that arrogance for what it is: the raw edge of a fiercely engaged will, the intention to completely dominate.

The sad truth is that in this country we are peculiarly vulnerable since our national identity seems to have faded away. We are fumbling for a new image because we have, perhaps, lost the drive and conviction which produces one organically. So we have strayed into the great waxwork hypermarket to choose a dummy and unfortunately our attention has been caught by the most fraudulent of Disney figures. Mickey, alias Uncle Sam, is beckoning. He is calling to us in that smarmy, cloying voice – he is already dictating our letters.

17. Sick-list Cyclist

Current cycling is increasingly concerned with issues of sickness and health. Our latter-day Lazarus, Lance Armstrong, has lain in the tomb undergoing devastating chemotherapy before shrugging off divine intervention to call himself forth by his own superhuman will. Not only that, he has out-classed mere resurrection by winning four Tours on the trot. As a real-life fable it beats St John's Gospel by thousands of kilometres. It also conveniently draws attention away from the drug-crazed hysteria of the rest of the *peloton*. We are clinging to our Lazarus reborn as tightly as pilgrims to Lourdes hug their bottles of holy water. Cycle sport has dug its own grave so wide and so deep that only a miracle can save it from toppling in, and Lance is that miracle. But for how much longer?

All human beings tread a fine line between sickness and health, but for competitive cyclists the marker is almost imperceptible. They push their bodies and their minds so fiercely that they place themselves at abnormal risk. From the great champions down, they have always been subject to nagging and major debilities. Louison Bobet spent years chafing a large cyst in the saddle area before he had it removed late in his career. It was said of Coppi that he had bones of glass, he broke so many and so often. There are also incidental ravages attendant upon the celebrity spotlight. Hugo Koblet caught VD while on a ceremonial participation in the Tour of Mexico which put an end to his golden period. Greg Lemond nearly finished himself off in a shooting accident. Rates of suicide and early death are significantly higher than for ordinary mortals and are rising steeply in the present climate.

As professional athletes expected to perform at the highest level, the top riders are, of course, more preoccupied than normal with their state of health – and this goes right down through the hierarchy. Robert Millar has reported how obsessive the ACBB coaches were about their charges keeping a cap on even in a car and never opening the windows for fear of a draught and a resultant cold. That 'strip-down and scrub plus a fresh tee-shirt' which we see the winner receive after a classic is a glimpse of the same meticulous school of thought and practice. As well as the nagging little complaints like head-colds, sinusitis, conjunctivitis, a touch of bronchitis needing antibiotics (which seems to happen a lot or serves as a handy excuse in many circumstances), saddle soreness and the avoidance of boils (Stephen Roche always insisted on washing his own shorts for this very reason) – there are also the longer-term, more deep-seated debilities due to general wear-and-tear like glandular fever. Our own David Millar has suffered, as did Eddy Merckx. But the king of the hill in this division is, of course, Lance Armstrong, who continued to race with advanced cancer.

Paradoxically, super form can often display all the signs of the onset of illness: pallor, sunken cheeks and a certain torpor off the bike; but as soon as our malingerer sits in the saddle he commands the vigour of a tiger. Jean Bobet recounts in his memoirs how Louison complained of not feeling well on the crucial Mont Ventoux stage of the 1955 Tour.

'I knew then that he would do a good ride,' was his brother's wry comment. And he did, dropping the 'Angel of the Mountains', Charly Gaul, to take the stage thus setting himself up for his hat-trick victory.

There have also been remarkable recoveries: Museeuw, of recent years, fighting back from a threatened amputation; Pantani surmounting a complicated fracture to win the Tour; Joop Zoetemelk who fractured his skull in 1974 and having recovered to win Paris–Nice in '75 then caught a life-threatening bout of meningitis but held on for a further 12 years to take the Amstel Gold at the age of 40. Greg Lemond rose above his own setback to win another two Tours. It must be said, however, that the ones who didn't recover are perhaps too easily forgotten. The comeback of Wilfried Nelissen (who, shortly after Pantani's fracture, broke his leg) though bravely engaged, failed to restore him to his previous level. Roger Rivière, the most talented rider of his generation, plunged into a ravine during the '59 Tour and lived the rest of his life in a wheelchair. But all in all, the image of cycling remains one of resplendent fitness and formidable athleticism no matter what clouds have gathered on the horizon of recent years.

I dwell on these matters now with a fascination bred of aged infirmity. My own little career has often fluctuated disastrously between health and sickness. Looking back over decades of highs and lows, I'm amazed at how robust I was in my clubrun days. Up and out in all weathers, sometimes drenched to the bone; sucking in the frosty air of a winter's morning while twiddling a low-fixed wheel – what was wrong with me then? Not a thing. I once even overshot a hairpin bend on a descent and plunged over the hedge into a grassy ravine with no more damage than multiple bramble scratches. The oblivious, charmed existence that most of us lead was mine too; I was a force of nature, indestructible.

Curiously enough, I had been a rather sickly child. Every year I spent at least a week in bed with some kind of fever. The root of the problem was judged to be my tonsils and at the age of 11 I had them out. From then on those yearly indispositions seemed to melt away and as I was drawn into cycling, especially the Sunday runs, I became phenomenally healthy. My mother would often deplore the shattered state I arrived home in. 'You're killing yourself on that old bike,' she would say at the door, but the opposite was the case.

This state of grace held through my university years and into full-time employment. It was only in the later stages of my drinking and driving years that I began to suffer again from some yearly malaise, usually a cold settling on the chest and needing antibiotics. Then on holiday in Rome just before the axe fell, I awoke a few nights with a tight chest – probably due to too many espressos – and immediately diagnosed myself as asthmatic. When I got home I chivvied my GP into prescribing the latest wonder inhaler. Although I hadn't much time for the industry or its methods, we all believed in the efficacy of drugs in those days, they would cure everything. Quite the reverse was true, however; that puffer set me on the road to Chronic Obstructive Airways Disease. As a parting gift, the drug barons had taken revenge, they had slipped me their trademark black spot.

Over the next few years of anguish, at my wits' end to retrieve my declining fortunes, I began losing weight and suffering long periods of some unspecified debility. One morning I found myself coughing specks of blood and immediately assumed that I had lung cancer. After an X-ray, I was summoned to the local hospital where I learned that it was only TB. Nothing serious – just nine months on antibiotics, no isolation hospital, not even time off work. I was so relieved that I took off at full pelt on my bike to bring home the good news. The final corner came up too soon and my braking was found wanting. I nearly went under the front wheels of an oncoming car. I laughed in the face of the terrified driver. What could touch me, I was invulnerable – hadn't I just survived cancer?

On a subsequent check-up, the chest physician expressed some concern that I rode everywhere in London's polluted atmosphere. I brushed his reservations aside, assuring him that I felt fine, but there was undoubtedly something in what he said. Much of the gradual deterioration in my respiratory system can be traced to a determination to keep on cycling, especially to and from work, whatever the conditions.

Soon after I finished the antibiotics, my mother died and I inherited the family home. This gave me a roof over my head and a small income from the top flat. A kind of convalescence had dropped into my lap. From then on I decided to lead a modest life at home. I was 'trying to write', as they say – another serious infection. Ever since I left university I had been scribbling on the side in expectation of breaking through as a gritty playwright like John Osborne or Dennis Potter.

The literary life proved hard graft, however. I was, of course, over-ambitious, intent upon immediate glory and it just didn't happen, or even any whiff thereof. Every now and then I would sink into such a trough of depression that there seemed no alternative but to seek honest employment. There followed a sequence of teaching jobs, attended by bike, which ended inevitably in bronchitis – or worse.

Then in early 1977 my girlfriend fell pregnant and I was forced back onto the job market in earnest. Lots of avenues were closed to me, certainly teaching, so I opted to retrain as a book-keeper on what was called a 'TOPS' course. Fatally I had little interest in book-keeping but there seemed to be a demand for part-time practitioners which would leave me a margin of freedom. I still hadn't learned the real lesson though: that winter-commuting on a bike was a health hazard. As soon as the weather got bad, so did I, with the usual chest infection. My last-chance career seemed to be slipping away. In desperation I took to wearing a mask – one of those old industrial-cum-smog versions made of cotton wool and shiny alloy. People would see me coming from afar and stand stock-still to watch me pass. They became shameless ghouls thinking that I had some awful injury with a bandage round my chops. Masks have caught on since, I'm glad to say, because the pioneering days were purgatorial.

I limped to the end of the course, broken in wind and mind, never wanting to hear the word 'book-keeping' again, much less practise it.

After such a disastrous entry to the '80s, I began to haunt the hospital chest clinic until they took me in for a week of tests. I was put to bed with another mask, a plastic one with a little fountain which played soothingly once the oxygen was turned on. I was told to indulge this delightful ritual three times a day and take a small tablet every morning. The first night I plumbed unfathomed depths of sleep and awoke famished. I began to eat like a Tour rider, seconds of everything.

'When would the tests begin?' I asked.

'Later in the week, we've got to prepare you first,' they said. I didn't care, I was quite content with my NHS hookah and its moist Swiss-mountain air. Life was suddenly delightful, abundant with promise. I found that I was free to come and go as I pleased so I made a daily excursion to South Kensington Tube and environs which reminded me of school days. I would browse in bookshops, buy extra treats for teatime and often sit down to a supplementary snack. It seemed absurd that I should be in hospital and feel so well. All the worry and concern of the last few years had blown away like the fine mist in my nebuliser mask.

This idyll was soon brought to a close. I found myself subjected to an afternoon of lung-searing tests. When I got back to my bed the bottle and mask had been removed, but I was still in such good spirits that it didn't matter. I went home on the crest of the wave that had been building for a week, confident that all my problems were behind me. Unfortunately, my euphoria gradually ebbed away over the next few days so that after a week I was back to my crumpled, anxious self. Withdrawal symptoms had set in with the realisation that the uplift would not be permanent. However, some survival instinct had prompted me to secrete away one of the nebuliser masks while still in hospital (they were thrown out anyway). In desperation I went to my GP and beseeched him for an oxygen bottle. But he took cover behind the hospital; I was under their care now. When I went along for my next appointment, I determined to throw myself on their mercy, anything at all for that daily pick-me-up, my future life depended on it.

I was confronted by a fat-jowled young registrar who gave me a stern dressing-down for wasting the hospital's time and resources. My tests were fine, there was nothing wrong with me at all. What I needed was to pull myself together and get a job.

Shock and bewilderment prevented me from suggesting that of course my tests were okay, I was high on bronchodilators and steroids. The weight of the condemnation overcame me: I was just a wretched malingerer, there could be no appeal. I slunk away down corridors which I had so recently explored with fascinated delight, a hopeless case, sentenced to unrelieved ill health in perpetuity.

Then there was the pottery.

The implacable voice of authority had spoken: get a job. So I took the only one on offer. My poor old moth-eaten bellows were offered up to the dust chamber of the potter's studio. The very thought of it made my bronchial tree shrivel up in fear, but I had to pull myself together and see it through. The air was thick with a fine white powder which made my throat look like a hole in the snow when I caught sight of it in the evenings. No matter, I told myself, redemption is only fully available in the most difficult of circumstances. Lost to sense or reason, I was intent upon breaking through the cycle of recurrent illness at any price – even if it should cost me my health. Like the medical establishment, I had come to believe that the sickness was all in my head. Dragging myself there every day like a gradually fading ghost, I found it more and more difficult to even manage the long flight of stairs up to the Tube platform. There was no question of riding, this was the last gasp.

In the end, of course, I collapsed completely, and was rushed to the local hospital in the middle of the night. On the stretcher I found myself clamped onto my old friend, a nebuliser mask. When the ward round loomed up beside my bed the next morning enquiring how I felt, the words stuck in my throat and I burst into tears. Within a few days though, I was back on my feet and just as I was settling into the routine they sent me home.

Reflecting on it all in the cool light of recovery, I began to realise that my derangement might have been due, in some distant way, to ideas I picked up as a teenage cyclist – the code of the iron will, for instance, the notion that the mind must override the body; that strenuously cultivated self-discipline which has an undoubted positive influence, but which can also spill over into delusion. Look at Lance Armstrong: still racing with advanced cancer – or Robin Buchan dead on his bike in the '70s trying to sweat off 'flu, or the tragedy of Tom Simpson. My demoralised and depleted state had reduced me to primitive reactions; it was almost as if I had reached a point where I was pleading to be put back on my bike.

By no small miracle I have since been able to ride my bike regularly, even riding a short distance to work with the help of a mask in winter, but always carefully, aware finally of the risks I might be running.

In the summer of 2000, in mid-July, there came a Saturday morning of bright sunshine and blue skies which offered itself as a perfect gift for a ride. I doubted if it would hold into the afternoon, but it did and left me with no excuse. My rides that year had been few and far between and rather clouded with after-effects, but I couldn't help feeling that everything would be put to rights on such an afternoon. I was utterly wrong. In spite of the benevolent conditions, I struggled all the way to Richmond Park with a splinter of ice in my chest which refused to melt. Once there, seated on a little bench below the Royal Ballet school, I hoped to at least enjoy the achievement, but nothing within me warmed. Instead, I realised that the weather, the luscious greenery and the sense of space were pressing in upon me like a reproach, a burden; that I had no place there, that for me it was all over. I told myself, in that numb condition, to accept it with good grace – not to make a fuss, no announcements, but to leave the bike where it usually stands and let it be. The decision was final and binding, there was nothing more to do but ride home.

I was as good as my word, we went on holiday bikeless, but that was as expected. And then, one Sunday in late August, the telephone rang – it was Bo. He was calling to announce that he was about to ride up from Crawley to visit me. This was astounding news. Hilda had written some time before saying that she had prevailed upon him to seek treatment for the lapses of memory and blackouts which were affecting him more and more, so a ride of such a nature was unbelievable.

Bo's fate had been a tragic epilogue to the Westwelve story. In 1961 he crashed at Reading track while teaching a club-mate the rudiments of track craft. His skull was fractured and he spent a week on the danger list. Hilda recounted how she thought he was dying. He was transferred to the Radcliffe Infirmary in Oxford and there began to recover, but it was a long haul. Eventually he was able to resume work and the whole family moved to Crawley where he and Hilda raised three exemplary children. The terrible irony was that he who had given so much to the game, had inspired so many others, should have suffered so grievously because of it.

All that morning I was concerned about his progress and whether he would make it at all. Just after lunchtime though, the doorbell rang and there he was smiling triumphantly, the old Bo, with a helmet on and some unlikely towelling shorts. His bike was a rather heavy production-line Peugeot; the equipment fetishist had given way to a more relaxed attitude.

When we sat down in the garden, he dropped his bombshell: 'These tablets I've been taking must really have done me good, I managed to climb Reigate Hill.' This was the kind of announcement which creates havoc within, the news that travels through the bloodstream asking each limb and organ: 'Could *you*, would *you* be able?' Reigate Hill with its sapping gradient and unending progress upwards; one of the ultimate tests of all that the bike demanded – and that among today's teeming traffic. I could not but admire him for his resilience and fortitude; he was still doing what I could only write about, it was amazing.

My wife and I fussed about, offering food and drink while Bo jubilantly filled in the details of his epic. It was the old runs captain again centre stage, commanding attention with his appetite for life. He was overwhelming us, so I decided to call up reinforcements. Chris was glad to be extricated from some

DIY task and shot round immediately.

There we were then, gathered around the table: Chris and I inclined towards the past, Bo exuberantly fixed on the present. His memory was still a bit shaky, but he had definitely regained his old charisma. In fact, it occurred to me that Chris and I were, in a sense, back beside that road in the Chilterns circa 1954 – looking on like awestruck schoolboys.

That visit renewed my faith, brought me back to the wisdom of keeping an open mind. I was set upon renouncing the saddle for ever, yet I continued to ride my shopping bike. We love striking grand poses, especially to ourselves. We like to think we can dispose our lives how we see fit, but really we have little power or control. Something still and certain assured me that my options remained open, that I should simply wait and see. In the meantime, I could always go back to the home trainer.

179

18. Bikie

Even as she touched down from the long night-flight of dreams, Barbara knew that something was wrong. Instinctively she sought her husband's reassuring presence, but met instead a sharp, cold edge. She froze, though her hands dutifully continued their search. Again they registered the same forbidding contact. Barbara came to herself in a sudden rush; she gripped the duvet, and tumbling out onto the floor, drew it with her to stand and confront this strange bedfellow. The sight made her rise up onto her toes and gasp. There laid out beside her was a bright orange bicycle.

'*Geraaald*,' she screamed until, out of breath, she began to sob.

Her two daughters came charging through the door almost immediately.

'What's the matter, Mum? Why's that bike in the bed? Where's Dad?' The questions rattled out, one after another.

'You'll have to ask him, wherever he is,' said Barbara. 'Gerald,' she barked now, sternly, 'Gerald.' He must show himself and come to justice. This was incredible even by his cracked standards. He lived and breathed ruddy cycling, but he had never gone so far as to bring a bike to bed. 'Gerald,' her voice rose again to outrage. 'Come here this minute.'

They stood, all three, listening intently for guilty scurryings from the rest of the house, but no sound came.

It was then that Barbara noticed his old winter jacket on the back of the chair, with the tracksuit bottoms that formed the rest of his dressing gown. They had been there all along.

To smother the small catch of a new apprehension, she swept around to the other side of the bed to make sure. She even looked under it. There, in place, were the fur-lined cycling shoes – another relic – which served him as slippers.

The girls were enthralled by the urgency of her search, but Barbara didn't want to be watched. She shooed them out the door. 'Go downstairs and look for your father. Check if his bike's there – and the car,' she said.

Once they had gone, she returned to the wardrobe and went through his suits, his shoes. Everything was undisturbed, even his watch on the bedside table. Her hands were suddenly icy. To distract herself, she turned back towards the bed to inspect the bicycle.

There was something old-fashioned about it, even she could tell that. In spite of its drop handlebars, it wasn't a real racer. The fat tyres, the mudguards and the saddlebag – nobody had those any more. It was a schoolboy's mount, a first grown-up bike, she felt certain. But who was it for then? And why had he put it in the bed? Her eyes were drawn to the deep orange lustre of the paintwork. There was a feeling of newness about the whole thing, an uncanny freshness as if the wrapping paper had just been taken off. She noticed that the tyres had a curious bloom on them, like grapes; surely they had never been ridden?

There weren't even any grease marks on the sheets. And as she leant over to make a closer inspection, she became aware of its distinctive smell, a mixture of lubricating oil, new leather and fresh paint – a strangely soothing aroma. It left no mark at all – how could that be? Perhaps every one was like that when they came off the assembly line, as bright and shining as newborn babies. But her bed was a long way from any factory gate or even a shop. The mystery deepened at the same time as the certainty grew that the bike itself held all the answers. There it lay, dumb and helpless, offering itself in seeming innocence. How had it fetched up between her sheets like some huge stillborn insect, with its hollow criss-cross body, its skinny arms and legs, its peculiar bent-over head, all horns?

A soon as they heard her cry, the girls raced back up again. Barbara was crumpled beside the bed sobbing uncontrollably. After a while, they put the arms around her and comforted her in the same way that she had always comforted them.

Though he lay still, Gerry was alive with a blissful tingling which was both confirmation and promise that all his dreams were coming true. He had embraced them in the same firm grip with which they now embraced him. No memory remained of his transformation besides the overwhelming fact that this exhilaration was fixed for ever.

Somewhere in the depths of sleep, he had found himself pounding home from the clubrun to watch the finish of the Tour on TV – and suddenly he was whisked away to the winner's rostrum on the Champs-Elysées. They were fitting him with the *Maillot Jaune*. For the first time in the illustrious history of the race, a fan had won; and it was a just and clear-cut victory. Of all the millions who followed the great spectacle, devouring press reports, religiously tuning in to every scrap of TV coverage; of all the multitudes who lived and breathed every pedal turn during the feverish month of July, *his* devotion and commitment had proved the strongest. Because the Tour was bigger than the riders, bigger than the great rolling extravaganza of the race caravan, bigger even than the international media explosion; it was a focus for a whole world of dedicated enthusiasts who, like himself, participated in this yearly exaltation of pedal power – but only from the sidelines. By snatching such an unexpected victory he had broken through the barriers, let them in to the action. From now on they all stood a chance of mounting the podium.

The jubilant afternoon gave way to a triumphal return to England where he was fêted on all sides. During a ceremonial visit to a cycle factory, however, he found himself tripping on the rim and plunging into a vat of molten steel which was about to be drawn off as tubing for bike frames. Immediately his golden progress became a hellish ordeal. He was subjected to every rigour known to the hardened roadman: from the tar-melting heat of the high mountains to blizzard days on Belgian cobbles. In between times there would be the spur of a blowtorch urging him on for another Hot-Spot sprint. His mettle was tested to the limit, and then beyond. But he knew in his indomitable stayer's heart that he must suffer through to the finish; for that was what he called upon when the going got tough: suffering. And suffer through he did until he was purged of any excess, tempered down to the bare essentials. At last he was given the sunlit coat of immortality. It was baked onto his shoulders as an enduring memorial to his greatness. For he was greater than the great now, not just in achievement and standing, but in his very essence – he was that essence.

When Barbara got back from dropping the girls at school, she was still clinging to the hope that it had all been some ghastly hallucination, that when she went up she would find her husband curled beneath the covers.

On the stairs, her heart thumped away mocking her timid footfalls.

He was still there, where she had left him, lying in state. There would be no let out, no reprieve; she would have to confront the reality.

'But why?' she found herself groaning aloud, 'Why?'

After so much mystification and confusion, she was stunned at the speed of the response; it came back like a shaft of light hitting a mirror – so swiftly that she sank to her knees and began to cry. There was no doubt, no reservation: *he had been going that way for years.*

The tears blotted out all thought and after a while she felt better. Everything became clearer. He had deserted them; it happened all the time in one way or another. He'd got so bound up in this cycling thing that it had taken him over. She felt sure that he was happy with her, with the girls and their life together, you couldn't have found a happier man. It was perhaps his happiness that had spirited him away. She would just have to carry on. What else could she do?

She drew herself up, went to the bed and lifted him onto the floor. He was surprisingly heavy, more substantial than all that finery in the garage – smaller too, more her size. In the early days she had ridden a bit, she had even enjoyed their runs together. But then the girls came along.

The tears came welling up again so she wheeled him over by the window and began to straighten the bed.

It had all started in earnest when he got the branch managership and persuaded them to install a shower during the refit of the office. From then on he was able to ride to work and that did him enormous good. He kept saying how much better he felt, how many more miles he was getting in. Before long he started racing again and it was his idea to go to France for the *randonnée*. She remembered how radiant he looked when he came back and how he implored her to come along on the next, just for the trip. She went reluctantly and had a great time. Oh, those long weekends while they were off riding, just sitting around nattering with Gloria and Betty. What a laugh they had . . .

She sat on the bed again to hold back the tears.

Those visits to France really transformed their lives. She had started work again at the car rentals, though she didn't have to, but it gave them more money for the trips. They went everywhere: Italy, Spain, Belgium. Then the girls started tagging along and the next thing they wanted lightweights to join in the runs. After that he began to get more kids interested in the club, he became the unofficial youth officer. Helen was his first big triumph. He'll miss her joining the World Class Performance Plan next year. But maybe that doesn't matter to him where he's gone.

He loved the fellowship and respect that cyclists enjoyed over there – and the food, the wine, it was a whole new world. How they would miss him, he'd made as many friends on that side of the Channel as he had on this. His enthusiasm was infectious, they all said he was the best thing that had ever happened to the club. When old Brian died he was certain to be president.

Of course there was something kinky about the way he doted on those bikes, it was like him having a harem under the family roof. But even that died away a bit when he got into organising and promotion. Anyway, she could allow him some indulgence as he was so devoted in all other departments.

'Bikie' was his pet name for himself; they were all bikies down the club. There was something childish about it, but that's men for you. They did enjoy themselves, though, they all enjoyed themselves. Once it opened up more to the women, some of them even started riding again. She would have joined in herself but Gloria and Betty preferred drinking, they weren't interested in exercise. 'I get enough of that round the house,' Betty said, so she hadn't bothered.

Bathed in floods of sunlight from the window, the orange paintwork really shone. What was it about orange that so entranced him? There was a reason and she had heard it time and again as she had heard everything in the long saga of his cycling history. All his bikes had been orange except the carbon thing – that had cost over eight hundred pounds, just the frame. She'd wanted a new settee for the front room, but he had to have it. She got the settee the next Christmas, though. He'd landed an even bigger bonus. You couldn't say his work suffered, quite the reverse; he was doing better and better on all fronts.

Wasn't it something to do with that picture on his side of the bed, the one of Eddy Merckx? She twisted round to look up at it. He couldn't get enough of 'the cannibal', as he called him, the greatest champion of all time. She could hear his voice and the special reverential tone it took on . . . 'the cannibal'. And instantly it came back to her.

She stood up and turned towards the window. 'Because his first bike had been the same colour,' she intoned softly to herself as if she couldn't quite understand the meaning of the words. 'That's what you shared with the great Eddy, the special Malteser orange of his bikes . . . ' Then she rushed across to kneel before the bike, tears rolling down her cheeks again. 'You've gone back to where it all started, your first bike – that's it, isn't it?'

Wiping away the tears as she did so, she began to stroke the saddle, the top tube, the forks with her moistened fingers as if to soothe and console him. There was even a slight tingling in her fingertips, like pleasant static. Then suddenly that smell came again, so fresh, so tangy – the smell of something just born. All at once she felt the warmth of the sunshine on her face and heard herself crooning over a bike in an upstairs room. What must she sound like?

As she stood up, leaning on saddle and handlebars for support, a great sigh escaped her and she took a deep breath of the air from outside, heard the birds chirruping in the trees while beneath her hands she could feel the crisp twill of handlebar tape and shiny untried leather. All these benign sensations began to fuse into a light-hearted decision. She found herself manoeuvring towards the door. The stairs might present a problem, but she would manage, as she would manage everything now. It felt as if she had grasped a new and delightful freedom, the chance to go out for a ride herself – on her own new bike.

For Gerry the quintessence of his fixation was revealed. His steadfast contentment made for a glorious transport: he bore and was borne. The tingle of anticipation had found its touch like a grounded tuning fork and its exquisite resonance coursed through him. He was both soloist and chorus, triumphant in all his parts. He had come at last into his own, his element; he was singing the song of the open road – he *was* that song.